HYPERLEARNING

HYPERLEARNING

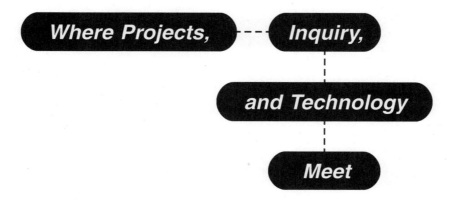

Where Projects, Inquiry, and Technology Meet

Jeffrey D. Wilhelm

and

Paul D. Friedemann

with

Julie Erickson

Stenhouse Publishers

York, Maine

Stenhouse Publishers, 431 York Street, York, Maine 03909
www.stenhouse.com

Library of Congress Cataloging-in-Publication Data
Wilhelm, Jeffrey D., 1959–
    Hyperlearning : Where projects, inquiry, and technology meet / Jeffrey D.
  Wilhelm and Paul Friedemann with Julie Erickson.
        p.   cm.
    Includes bibliographical references (p.   ).
    ISBN 1-57110-054-7 (alk. paper)
    1. Interactive multimedia—United States—Authoring programs.
  2. Hypertext systems—United States. 3. Computer-assisted instruction—United
  States. 4 Instructional systems—United States—Design. I. Friedemann, Paul. II.
  Erickson, Julie.
  III. Title.
  LB1028.55.W55 1998   98-16523
  371.33′475′92—dc21   CIP

Cover and interior design by Ron Kosciak, Dragonfly Design
Typeset by Technologies 'N Typography

Manufactured in the United States of America on acid-free paper
03 02 01 00 99 98 9 8 7 6 5 4 3 2 1

First, this one's for my dad, who teaches by example.

Next, it's for all of those who have taught me through their own writing, primarily Stuart Greene, George Hillocks, Brenda Power, and Denny Wolfe.

Jeff

This is for my dad and mom, Don and Mary Friedemann, and in memory of Lois Weingarten, my first-grade teacher, who told me I was a great writer.

Paul

Contents

Acknowledgments · ix

Introduction · 1

1 · Where We Are and How We Got Here · 5

2 · The Promise of Hypermedia · 15

3 · Situating Our Teaching: Constructivism, Cognitive Apprenticeship, and Student Design · 27

4 · Setting It Up: Getting Kids into the Flow of Hypermedia Design · 39

5 · Beginning the Inquiry Process · 63

6 · Dealing with Information · 91

7 · Into the Lab: Designing Hyperstacks and Creating Critical Scoring Guides · 109

8 · Getting It Right · 137

9 · Into the Future · 159

Works Cited · 169

Acknowledgments

There are always many people to acknowledge and thank for their support during a project such as this, which was nearly a decade in the making. Thanks to everyone who guided and supported us; you know who you are, and you know we appreciate your help.

In particular, I would like to thank Richard Lehrer and Julie Erickson of the University of Wisconsin. They introduced us to the notion of teaching with hypermedia and assisted, cajoled, and challenged us throughout the years of our work with design-centered learning. The teaching described here would have been impossible without their expertise and guidance.

Thanks to Anne Haase, whose prior work with hypermedia was of great help to us.

Thanks are always due to my wife, Peggy Jo, and my daughters, Fiona and Jasmine, for inspiration, understanding, encouragement, and fairly continual indulgence.

Thanks, of course, to Paul for being a great friend, colleague, and teacher. When others say something cannot be done, Paul is often out there already doing it. He is positive, honest, direct, and willing to hang himself out over the yawning gulp for the good of his school, students, and friends. He is the ultimate team-teaching partner.

I'm very appreciative of my friends at Beaver Dam Middle School and the Unified District, particularly Bob Hanson, Craig Martin, Jeff Duchac, Brian Ambrosius, Judy Bovee, Erv Barnes, Jackie Burke, and Nancy Cook. Their collegiality, professionalism, and support continue to be important.

I'd like to acknowledge the mentorship of many past and present teachers and colleagues: Bill Anthony, Leon Holley, Jr., Michael Smith, John Thorpe, Jim Chiavacci, Paula Moore, Jan Kristo, Brenda Power, Rosemary Bamford, Stuart Greene, Denny Wolfe, Bill Strohm, James Blaser, and Jack Wilhelm.

And finally, my thanks to all the wonderful students with whom I have designed and learned.

Jeff

First, I thank my best friend and wife, Jane Friedemann. Jane's encouragement, understanding, and English skills were, and are, invaluable to me.

I thank Jeff for the constancy of his friendship, the contagious nature of his energy, and his devotion to bringing the best to all his students.

I acknowledge all my friends and colleagues at Beaver Dam Middle School and the Unified District for the support, inspiration, and example they provide me. I especially thank Craig Martin, Brian Ambrosius, Robin Peters, Jeanne Frick, Angie Kirst, Pat Miller, Jeff Duchac, Dennis McCormick, Judy Bovee, Bill Anciaux, Gene de Groot, and Dick Fitzpatrick.

I give special thanks to my classmates in the NLU masters program, notably Steve Anderson and Kurt Luedke, who shared their humor and commiserated with me through a Masters degree program that eventually led me to this book.

Finally, I would like to recognize all of my students for their hard work and their excitement for our projects. I am especially grateful for their willingness to help us with this book.

Paul

Introduction

In American classrooms, now and since the 19th century, teachers generally act as if students are supposed to learn on their own. Teachers are not taught to teach, and most often they do not teach. They assign and they grade but they do not instruct. The problem does not lie in individual incompetence or the incompetence of institutions. All participants in the educational enterprise share an inadequate vision of schooling. . . . Teaching must be redefined as assisted performance. Teaching consists in assisting performance. Teaching is occurring when performance is achieved with assistance.

Tharp and Gallimore (1990)

This book proposes to address the problem Tharp and Gallimore pointed out and to provide an antidote to it: inquiry-driven projects with technology, using a model we refer to as student-design learning (Lehrer, Erickson, and Connell 1994).

Our proposed solution is of interest and use to teachers in any situation. In fact, our most important argument, and the model of teaching that we espouse and demonstrate here, is quite general and widely applicable. We argue that design skills that are essential in the real world can be developed through short projects that can supplement traditional curricula in all subject areas.

We will have much to say to teachers who team-teach, teach in block schedules (or would like to), teach in an integrated fashion, or are searching for ways to integrate technology into their classes. We will also speak to those reconceiving their notions of literacy in an electronic age and who are interested in the new ways of knowing and composing offered by multimedia. For teachers who are not in these situations and do not have the freedom to pursue extended projects, this book will nevertheless provide an instructional model that can be used for shorter projects, for teaching individual skills and strategies both with and without technology with all kinds of compositions and ways of representing and demonstrating knowledge.

Chapters 5 through 8 provide specific advice for teaching particular skills of learning and design: collaborating, developing a sense of audience, asking questions, finding information, developing information, organizing and analyzing data, seeing patterns, categorizing, representing what has been learned, revising, and presenting. These skills and the instructional sequences we suggest will be informative, useful, and adaptable for all teachers. Although we use hypermedia as the end product for the projects we describe, the process is integral to all inquiry and all forms of representation.

However, there is no denying that we argue forcefully for a particular vision of education that is not widely practiced. We do not think that our vision is radical; in fact, it is supported widely by educational theory, research, and best practices in the field. Further, the changes we propose and have enacted do not require any kind of major overhaul to individual classrooms or the nation's schools.

What we do propose is that schools become reconceived as communities of practice, where students pursue personally relevant inquiry and create socially significant artifacts with other students, teachers, and members of the community. We think that these projects should be "real" in the sense that they are organized around truly contended and debatable issues that interest the students, require decisions and arguments to be made, and lead to some form of transformed understanding and social action.

To pursue this kind of curriculum, teachers will have to emphasize processes and ways of knowing, and will have to reconceive how time is spent in schools. We contend that important life skills for learning can be mastered only over time through multiple levels of assistance provided by the expertise of the teacher, through peers, and ultimately through self-assistance.

The thinking and projects described in this book are the result of eight years of collaboration and experimentation. There were trials and tribulations along the way, and we know that we have still further to go on our teaching journeys. But as we once heard Eric Johnson, an educational consultant, say, all educational experiments are doomed to succeed—except on Friday afternoons and during the whole month of February! We agree and know that even when things didn't go as we would have liked, we and our students learned more about teaching and learning as a seamless and unified act.

A couple of notes on the book: All of the anecdotes and teaching and learning events we describe here are real. All the work examples are from students. Most of the students are composites, and all names are pseudonyms.

We start each chapter with a list of important points made in the chapter. This list is not exhaustive, but provides a general road map for your reading. The book moves generally from an overview of important issues regarding technology and education, to a theoretical discussion that informs how we can usefully think about these issues and implement new kinds of teaching, to a close look at our own practice in our classrooms. To provide specific electronic examples of classroom work that supplement the figures we present in this book, we are maintaining a web site at the URL www.nconnect.net/~frito. We encourage readers to send us examples of their own students' work that might exemplify themes of this book.

In Chapter 1 we provide a general overview of the purposes of education and of learning with technology. Chapter 2 describes hypermedia and explains what students learn by creating their own hypermedia documents. We explain how the use of such projects is supported by recent calls for more integrated and inquiry-based kinds of education.

Chapter 3 sets out the theoretical basis for the teaching described in this book. We explain how a clearly articulated theory of learning can help guide teaching. Then we outline the theory of constructivism and describe teaching models such as cognitive apprenticeship and student-designed learning that are highly specified, easily adapted to the classroom, and consistent with constructivist principles. *Readers who are more interested in practice than theory might want to read the later chapters that describe actual practice and return to this chapter later.*

Chapter 4 begins describing our classroom practice. We explain how to begin with short projects that can potentially lead to longer ones. We also show how traditional paper-and-pencil projects can easily be translated to hypercard form. We discuss sequencing both within and between units, and how one project can build skills, experience, and motivation for approaching the next project, which will be more challenging and sophisticated. This sequencing of projects can supplement traditional curricula or become an integrated, inquiry-based curriculum of thematic units focused on students' designing projects to answer their own questions.

Chapters 5 through 8 describe the process of helping students to develop specific target skills important to constructing knowledge across the curriculum. Chapter 5 is primarily about questioning and finding information. Chapter 6 focuses on analyzing and organizing the data students have collected during their inquiry. Chapter 7 highlights the design of hypermedia cards and stacks, and how to help students articulate and apply critical standards for assessing their projects. In Chapter 8, we discuss helping students to critique, reflect on, and revise their work.

Chapter 9 highlights how projects can be presented and used, and it concludes with a discussion of how the model of learning that organizes this book fosters a literacy of thoughtfulness and engaged learning that is essential in our current electronic age.

Chapter 1

Where We Are and How We Got Here

Important Points

➡ Technology is a means to an end, not an end in itself. Therefore, technology in schools must serve our higher educational purposes and the learning goals we have for students. Technology must help students develop foundational skills as readers, writers, thinkers, and learners.

➡ You don't need to know a lot about technology to use technology to teach. If you want to teach with technology, you *can* do it.

➡ Students need to learn how to learn. Technologies such as hypermedia can help by making how to learn and what is learned visible and accountable. By making learning visible, hypermedia can assist student performances in many foundational learning competencies, such as reading, writing, classifying, and organizing.

➡ Learning with technology is motivating and effective with all students, particularly those who are labeled or considered at risk.

➡ The student-design learning model uses technology to support student learning and help students to represent what they have learned to others. This model can be used with various technologies, such as video, or with other media, such as drama, bookmaking, and creating museum exhibits.

For a student who has a sufficient *why* to learn almost any *how* will do.

Neil Postman (1995)

If you want to really learn how to do something, you have to do it and keep on doing it. You have to like love doing it. If you want to really understand something, you have to kind of get inside it somehow.

Roper, seventh grader

Neil Postman, in his books *Technopoly* (1992) and *The End of Education* (1995), reminds us that often technology is used in schools as an end in itself, and not for developing powerful ways of thinking or familiarizing ourselves with powerful ideas. In other words, so-called educational technologies are not used as a way of becoming or being literate or of doing personally satisfying and socially responsive work. In schools, Postman writes, we are not using technology to serve our purposes; instead, technology is using us.

Students are put in the role of learning technology for its own sake. They do this instead of asking and then experiencing what fruitful human purposes may be served by mastery of the technology.

As we (Jeff and Paul) work with our own and other schools regarding teaching with technology, we often ask administrators about their districts' technology plans. They almost always reply with a wish list of hardware and software purchases. Teachers, when asked similar questions, often talk about the technology courses their school offers or is planning to offer. To us, these answers seem very far from the essential question of how important kinds of learning will be assisted through the use of technology. What we mean by the question about a "technology plan" is this: What vision do you have for how to use technology to help your students learn important, powerful, and flexible ways of learning and being in the world?

What's Essential and What's Not

What's essential is that students learn how to learn. To achieve this, they need to master foundational learning competencies such as reading, writing, and computation. (Later in this book, we will get to the nitty-gritty of how learning projects with hypermedia assist students to develop and extend these kinds of abilities, and we will provide detailed models and how-to instructions.)

Students also need to see and be able to set purposes for their learning. They need to know how to ask questions, find information, analyze and organize what they have learned, represent and revise their new and emerging understandings, and use these understandings to take action in the world. Later chapters in this book describe in concrete terms how hypermedia projects can help students to develop and powerfully use all of these strategies. We think of our own instruction as taking students from order to adventure. What we mean is that we assist students in highly structured ways to develop new skills, which they then come to use independently with self-directed projects of their own.

It is essential in any culture of learning that there are multiple models of real and enthusiastic learning, particularly from adults. We don't think most schools successfully provide these kinds of models. Throughout our recent teaching careers, we have tried to examine and learn from our own teaching practice and to make our learning processes and enthusiasms visible to our students. In the contexts we will describe, we have tried to model sound teaching, good learning, and powerful ways of demonstrating knowledge, such as good multimedia design. We have also taken on the roles of teacher-researchers who examined and critiqued, and attempted to improve our own practice. We view learning, demonstrating, critiquing, and teaching as related. Our hypermedia projects have helped us and our students to do all of these things, and they have provided all of us with a way to be both teachers and learners in and outside the classroom.

As teachers, we've also worked to model attitudes and ways to learn substantive content-area knowledge and ways to learn about computers. Neither of us has a computer background, and almost all of what we have learned about technology is from the context of our teaching. Although we have learned quite a lot over the years, we are both still technological neophytes in many ways.

Nevertheless, it's not important to know everything about technology to use it in your teaching. What is important is an attitude of inquiry—of recognizing problems and modeling the various ways of experimenting to overcome them. The world in general, and technology in particular, provide endless new challenges. We need to take up the challenges with our students, learn new skills, and talk about the difficulties and how (and if) they were overcome. (There have been many difficulties that we have never been able to solve, but that hasn't kept either of us from trying or from teaching well.) One essential way of teaching, after all, is to be learning something yourself—and if this learning is challenging and requires overcoming difficulties, then this is so much the better for your students.

This kind of learning is what this book explores, and we think that makes it fairly unique. This is a book about the interplay of teaching and learning with technology, particularly teaching and learning with hypermedia platforms. (If you want a book that is about technology or about particular hypermedia programs, there are plenty at your local bookstore.) A technology, after all, is simply an extension of natural human abilities. There's no need to fall victim to the "Gee Whiz!" syndrome when new technologies appear. Technologies like paper and pencil, the overhead projector, TV, and VCR are used and misused in schools every day.

The question that we want to take up is this: What are the special possibilities of computer technologies, particularly hypermedia platforms, for extending our abilities to teach and our students' inclination and abilities to learn? How can we use this technology to teach in a powerful way?

Really Among Schoolchildren

This book is made up of real-life teaching and learning experiences in classrooms of twenty-five to thirty children, yearly teaching loads of around 130 students, and a school with a single computer lab with outdated Mac Classic computers. We worked for many years in this situation as part of an integrated teaching team.

Throughout this book, "we" will refer to us—Jeff and Paul—who team-taught the learning projects described here as part of an integrated middle school teaching team.

In the midst of our development of extended learning projects using technology, we were joined for two years by Julie Erickson, a researcher studying children's thinking in classrooms. Julie, who has considerable expertise on teaching with technology, conducted her own research in our classrooms, helped us with our teacher research, and has contributed significantly to the writing of this book. When Julie figures in an anecdote, we refer to her by name.

We taught in the "house" (or "school within a school") that served all of our district's labeled students at the seventh-grade level. Any student with initials behind his or her name like LD (learning disabled), ED (emotionally disturbed), ADHD (attention deficit-hyperactivity disorder), or ESL (English as a second language) was in our "house," and they had all classes with the teachers in our house. (Houses and team teaching are middle school ideas that are gaining increasing credence in elementary and secondary schools.) We used to joke that our students' real problem was that they were "severely labeled" and that schooling is "teacher disabled." By that, we meant that the structures and strictures of school often worked against our attempts to innovate teaching responsive to our students' needs. Our colleagues also sometimes joked that we taught in the "outhouse" instead of a house.

What we found, though, was that students learn by doing, by making things of relevance that require them to use the skills they are learning, and by talking and reflecting about that learning and doing. Our own findings are widely corroborated in the research literature (Brown 1997; Brown and Campione 1996; Carver et al. 1992; Penner et al. 1997; Perkins 1986; Williams, Bareiss, and Reiser 1996). Students learn by being given the responsibility to design real artifacts that they can use to teach others significant ideas (Erickson 1997; Harel 1991; Harel and Papert 1991; Lehrer et al. 1994; Resnick and Ocko 1990). When we put our students, including the "severely" labeled ones, into this kind of learning situation, all of them shined. And those who were labeled or considered at risk seemed to thrive the most.

We began our respective work in schools as an English teacher/reading specialist (Jeff) and a social studies teacher (Paul). The first year that we were in the same building, we hardly knew each other because of the way most schools are organized, with teachers working alone to teach individual subjects, "delivering" or "transmitting information" from the mandated curriculum of that content area. As our school adopted a middle school model of education, teachers were put into teams and encouraged to develop integrated curriculum thematically organized around problems or patterns of ideas and that could be team-taught.

We were fortunate to be on the same team, because we were both beginning to think hard about the important issues that we will take up in this book. We began to develop instruction that would be informed by our current thinking, our theoretical orientations, and our past classroom experiences—and that we would scrutinize and revise as teacher-researchers. We have now worked together as teammates for six years, during that time developing the integrated hypermedia units described here. We also used the teaching frameworks (called *cognitive apprenticeship* and *student-design learning projects*) we describe here with projects that made use of drama, art, bookmaking, video projects, and creating museum exhibits and other low-technology media. (See Erickson 1997; Lehrer et al. 1994; Wilhelm 1996, 1997; Wilhelm and Edmiston 1998, for descriptions of these other kinds of work.)

Even as we began to team-teach, our classes met separately, although we often merged our classes into blocks (double periods in which students from social studies and reading/language arts worked together), or had students visit learning stations manned by us and other teachers instead of going to the assigned classroom for a particular period. These stations corresponded to the part of the project they were currently working on.

The kind of projects we espouse can work in self-contained classrooms in various disciplines, but they work particularly well in team-taught situations and with block schedules. It's also very helpful in such projects to solicit the aid of your librarian, parents, the community, other teachers, local experts, and any of a number of other people who, we have found, are very eager to help us.

A Generative Teaching and Learning Model

If this book were solely a specific how-to guide for using student-design learning projects with hypermedia, it would have some usefulness. We hope, however, that it goes beyond the specific descriptions of how to do particular kinds of work to provide a general and generative framework for using technology to learn and demonstrate new understandings.

We further hope that you will use and adapt this model, as we did, to inform various kinds of teaching. In other words, we think that our underlying ideas are far more adaptable and general than the necessarily focused examples and stories that we feature here. That's why we are highlighting some of these underlying ideas here and will develop them with concrete examples throughout the book.

The projects our students completed helped them to develop general strategies of learning and the ability to understand and self-manage these learning strategies independently. They also helped students to achieve specific literacy skills that they will use throughout their lives.

Designing hypermedia documents involves purposes and tools unique to electronic communication, which we believe will be important in the hypertextual future our students do and will continue to inhabit. In turn, this brings up the question of what it means to be literate in a technological age, a question we take up in our concluding chapter.

We use HyperCard (and sometimes HyperStudio) software in our work with students because these are highly adaptable, general-purpose softwares that can be used in a variety of situations and teach students a variety of skills and concepts useful in other computer environments. We also teach in such a way that the students are gaining cognitive skills. The use and understanding of generative cognitive skills is what we think makes up literacy. By "generative," we mean skills that are flexible and useful throughout life and lead to the refinement and development of other skills. For instance, if students possess the abilities to design artifacts that are of use for real audiences and they can use a variety of different *sign systems* (e.g., written text, visuals, graphics, video, body movement, music) or ways of making meaning to do so, then we believe that they have achieved literacy: the ability to continue learning, exploring, and communicating in communities of other learners.

Purposes and Themes of This Book

Through our classroom stories and instructional ideas, we will explore how to put an edge on teaching as "assisting student learning performances." We will examine how to provide real contexts and real audiences for student learning performances, in which learning and the resulting knowledge are purposeful, meaningful, and usable. We will look at learning as a social enterprise and at how to think of teaching as fostering democracy and joint productive activity among students and teachers. We will consider the nature of literacy and the new forms of literacy with which we all must contend in a technological and multimedia age. We ask, How can technology help us to know ourselves and the world? How does technological fluency relate to traditional forms of reading and writing? How might good learning habits with computers translate to good habits of learning in all walks of life?

We provide concrete how-to examples of instructing and learning that make use of hypermedia platforms to teach in new and more powerful ways, and will help students to develop foundational skills that they can then use on their own. We specifically look at how the context of hypermedia projects helped students develop the abilities to question, find and develop information, analyze and organize data, revise and represent what was learned, and use that new knowledge to take action in the world.

Telling the Whole Story

It's also important that we show some of the underside of our teaching story. As Thomas Newkirk (1992) points out, books and articles by some teachers overemphasize the positive and create a myth of Superteacher. These kinds of teacher stories puzzle and sometimes even disturb us. We find ourselves asking, Why does this teacher's experience not jibe at all with our own? Where in our classrooms is the kid who has his head on his desk and won't pay attention? Where are the kids who are pushing and shoving and banging on each other as they come into the room? Where are the kids yelling "This is STUPID!"? Where is the girl who is late and absent so much that you can't seem to keep her up with what the class is doing? Obviously we think our own teaching has been highly successful, or we wouldn't be writing a book about it.

Nonetheless, the course of true learning never did run smooth, and we will reveal not only our successes but the problems, obstacles, and hassles that we have overcome or still remain. This part of the story is the heart of action research, which asks: What can we do next to make things even better? Paul sometimes likes to joke that in our best moments we performed like "the Lennon and McCartney of teaching." We'd like to think this is true, but if it is, then we have also spent some time at the bottom of the quality charts wondering if we were destined to be one-hit wonders—kind of the educational correlative of Tony Orlando and Dawn!

Changing How We Teach

One final point is about values and the politics of changing how we teach. In the state where we teach together, there are nine general learning objectives or outcomes that every teacher must demonstrate they are pursuing with their own students, in whatever content area or grade level.

One year we received the list of outcomes and were asked to show how we were helping students to meet these objectives, which included ideas like "to become aware of and use various sources of information," "to become tolerant of other cultures and points of view," and so forth. Independently filling out the sheet, both of us wrote down "hypermedia cultural journalism project" for each of the nine outcomes.

We laughed when we talked about it afterward. "Everything the state wants our kids to know and do, we are teaching through this one extended unit," Paul rightly observed.

But when our reports were reviewed by department chairs and central administrators, we were called to a meeting and told that hypermedia *wasn't* part of our designated curriculum and therefore where were we getting off teaching it? The gist of our counterargument was that hypermedia was the tool we were using to develop the valued skills and concepts designated by our own curriculum and the state learning goals. We argued that values are inherent in the way that education is conducted, and that we were using hypermedia projects to teach in a way that was respectful of students and good for them, and that met the demands of our curriculum and state learning results.

We said that we were giving students control of the computer to create knowledge and to use it to teach others, rather than relying on sets of ready-made materials such as anthologies, textbooks, and premade tests. Our political argument was that "instructionist" or "information-transmission" teaching was not democratic, was disrespectful, and was, in fact, detrimental to our students. Our principal supported us, and we continued to refine and use our student-design projects in subsequent years, but the politics of changing the ways schools teach, even in small ways, was always very present for us.

We implicitly argue throughout this book that learning environments must be fitted to the nature of the child, and they must help the child to become more. Computers provide flexible environments for achieving this kind of growth that are far more consistent with what we know about children, about learning, and about effective teaching than traditional instructionist notions of teaching and preset curricula. It would be a great tragedy if computers were not used by students to pursue questions passionately and make things of personal relevance and social significance.

This is the challenge we take up here. It is not a light challenge, and we do not provide definitive answers. We do know, however, that we are on a journey in the direction toward more democratic and generative education, and we hope this book will help you on your own journeys.

School is a significant part of life for children, and it should be as powerful, engaging, and as meaningful as possible. But school is only part of a student's total life and must work to prepare her to become a democratic citizen and worker. We believe that students should experience the kind of learning and create the kind of documents, games, and ideas that they like to use and that they will be asked to use in the world of home and work in the not-too-distant future.

Students need to learn how to create knowledge and solve problems. We think they need to do less in order to do more (Brown and Campione 1994). Instead of learning a wide breadth of facts that they do not know how to integrate or use, as is typical in school curricula, they should engage in a few rich projects that support deep learning of both procedural knowledge and powerful ideas. These projects should work to develop firmly rooted cognitive skills by engaging students in deep reading, deep learning, and the deep engaging fun of constructing new understandings and creating new ways of representing what is being learned.

By learning deeply, students will learn how to learn. They will then be enabled—by gaining cognitive skills and learning how to think and learn for themselves—to learn anything in the future—a future that they can meet as their own.

Chapter 2

The Promise of Hypermedia

Important Points

This chapter describes hypermedia and explains what students learn by creating their own hypermedia documents. It explains how the use of such projects is supported by recent calls for more integrated and inquiry-based kinds of education.

➡ Hypermedia is a computer platform that communicates through nonlinear, multimedia text and is often composed by multiple authors.

➡ Hypermedia is the platform of the World Wide Web and will play an increasing role as a form of composition and communication.

➡ Hypermedia software is easy for teachers and students to learn and use.

➡ Student-created hypermedia projects can engage students of all interests and ability levels.

➡ Designing hypermedia projects encourages students to name themselves as readers, writers, and learners and supports them in the achievement of better reading, idea development, sense of audience, classifying, organizing, collaborating, representing understandings, revising, and articulating and applying critical standards about the quality of their work.

If you ask the kids to start designing hypermedia documents to develop knowledge and express what they've learned, don't expect to get a big Thank you or Hugs and kisses. After all, this is the real world and you're going to be requiring them to think.

Rich Lehrer, personal communication

This stuff [designing hyperstacks] is really hard. Why can't we just do worksheets?

Molly, seventh grader

You know, before this, I thought research was like going to the library and just copying things down and then handing in a report or reading it to someone. This hypermedia stuff we're doing makes me see that research is *real work* and that you have to learn things from lots of angles, and you have to actually create new knowings. Like, WOW, man!

Mike, eighth grader

I was in the computer lab and in a frenzy. I noticed that I was sweating, but I was too busy to care. After eight weeks of designing hyperstacks—electronic multimedia documents—that answered sophisticated research questions of interest to them, groups of seventh graders were critiquing their stacks and revising them for display at a school open house. I wondered if Paul was working this hard in his classroom as he helped another group of kids fine-tune their presentations for parents.

I had the distinct impression that I was somehow conducting class at the Chicago Board of Trade. There were papers everywhere—on the computer tables and strewn over the floor. Groups of students were huddled around computers. Kids were yelling to each other for help: "Who knows how to fix our drag animation?" "Who knows how to spell *restaurant*?" "How can we edit our button icons?" And, amazingly, other kids from different groups were gesturing to them or rushing over to help.

I had just moved from a group who wondered if their various hypercards worked together to provide a clear "central focus" regarding their research question about what visitors to Italy would most need to know to get along in that foreign culture. Although they had been through this several times before, I helped them to answer their own question through the use of an issue tree—a kind of concept web that shows the relationships of various ideas. (Chapter 5 provides a detailed explanation of how to make and use one.)

I then moved to a group that was wondering if the recent events in Rwanda and Burundi necessitated an update of their hyperstack about how the ethnic makeup of Africa would affect the future of that continent.

In the various groups, kids interrogated each other with the help of the assessment rubrics they had themselves created to ensure the quality of their hypermedia products (see Chapter 8). There were lots of animated discussions on an array of topics: how various readers would experience their hyperstacks, the numbers and quality of links between various hypercards, and the audiovisual and other creative features they had designed to help readers understand the importance of their research, among others.

Thirty students, including many bearing labels like ADHD, LD, or ED/BD, were all totally engaged. This energy surprised me continually during our cultural journalism unit, coming as it did from kids who would blow off quizzes and be satisfied with superficial work on more typical assignments. One such LD-labeled student, when asked why he was taking such care with an earlier design project, had told me, "I'm *making* this, and other people are going to see it!"

Mike, looking at the clock, excitedly informed his group that there were "only ten more minutes!" A huge groan went up; they had decided to add an interactive quiz to their hypermedia document, which they thought would help consolidate what their readers had learned from their stack. So at this point, they were hurriedly adding sound effect responses to their quiz—and running out of time. An emissary of the group was dispatched to ask me if I would stay after school so they could finish "this AWESOME talking quiz we are making."

"Why do you need this awesome quiz?" I asked. "Because it will make our stack work better! It'll remind people what they learned from it before they log off," I was told. I agreed to stay after school—for the third time that week. I smiled tiredly at the happy problem I was having.

Another group of girls was finishing their work. "We're done!" one exulted. They began to chatter excitedly about what they had learned from the project. "It's amazing to me," said Kristin, "how much work we did on this project and how cool it works!" When I asked why they had been motivated to do so much work, another girl told me that "it was about our own questions, so we were really interested. And we want other people to learn all about it too." In the course of their research about Africa, they had come across several health issues regarding women that they now felt passionately about. "People need to know about all of this," Kristin told me. "It's important. And we think we did a great job of helping anyone who reads this to know about it." A self-celebrating cheer went up from her group.

After eight weeks on the same project and lots of intense work developing skills like questioning, organizing information, and revising, the energy and positive feeling still ran high. The bell rang, kids hurriedly made their final revisions, and in a few moments all was quiet. I stood there in the sudden silence, tired in the marrow of my bones, but amazed at the work that can be done when students are creating something that they care about deeply.

What Is Hypermedia?

Hypermedia, like the scroll and medieval codex before it, is a new way of presenting ideas or "text" to communicate (Bolter 1991). Hypermedia consists of computer "cards," or screens, that can be filled with typed language information in the form of textual "fields," and filled—on its "background"—with pictures, photographs, drawings, graphics, video, music, other sounds, or animation. Cards are linked or connected to other cards through the use of "buttons." (See Figure 2.1.)

Hypermedia differs from a traditional book in two major ways. First, hypermedia is a multimedia text. It uses linguistic text in the form of words and joins these words with a high-tech combination of visuals and sounds. Second, hypermedia is nonlinear. Because of the button connections, a hypertext can be read in a variety of ways and sequences. Unlike a book, where the reader is expected to proceed from one page to the next, the reader of hypertext can proceed—theoretically at least—from any particular card to any other related card. A reader is not compelled to read the text in a particular order but can explore multiple associations in the way and order that makes sense to her or fits her unique purposes.

Because of this nonlinearity, separate hyperstacks can easily be combined with each other, because related features of one stack can be connected, or cross-linked, to related features of another stack (for example, the hotlinks, or buttons, on a web page lead the browser to related cards on other web pages). As a result, hypertexts tend to have multiple authors and contain multiple voices. Hypertextual authorship invites collaboration.

What Is Hypermedia?

Hypermedia is computer software for organizing and managing various types of multimedia information (text, graphics, animation, video, sound) into a system so that the user can easily access, retrieve, and modify the information.

The software programs make it possible to create what are basically stacks of index cards. The computer screen serves as the card and it can include multimedia information and be connnected or linked to any other cards in the stack.

The typical written document is linear. In other words it must be read in one way to get the information (Figure 1). A hypermedia document is a more nonlinear representation of information (Figure 2). Information can be structured in a hierarchy (Figure 3), a logical hierarchy (Figure 4), in a web (very rare) (Figure 5), or in some combination of these structures.

Figure 1 Linear structure

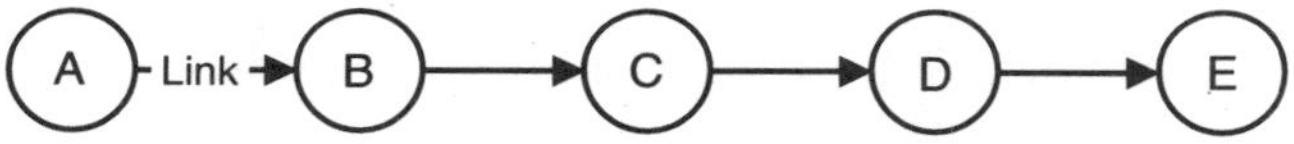

Figure 2 From the linear page to logical hierarchy

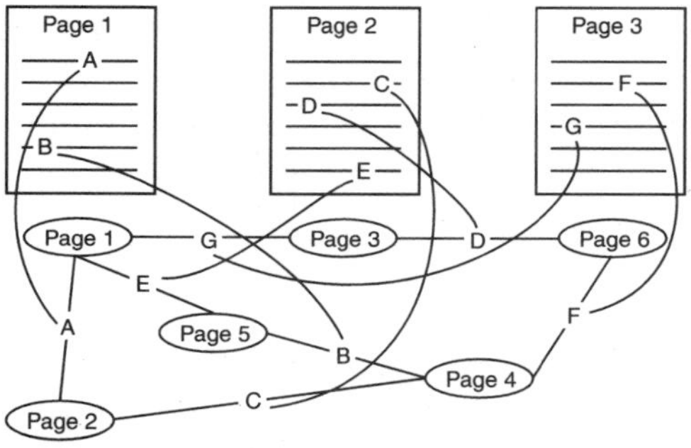

Figure 3 Hierarchical structure of information

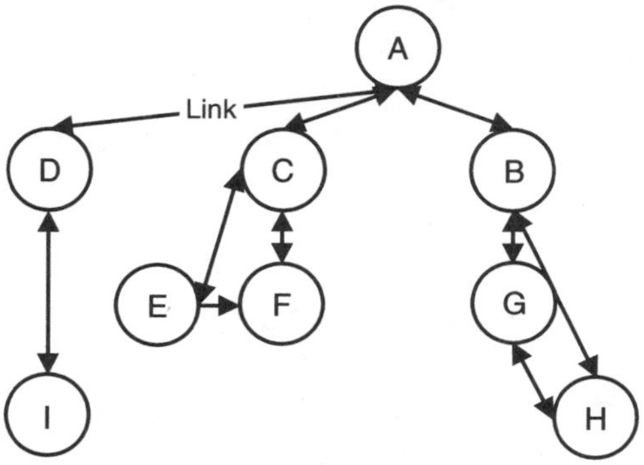

Figure 4 Logical-hierarchical structure of information

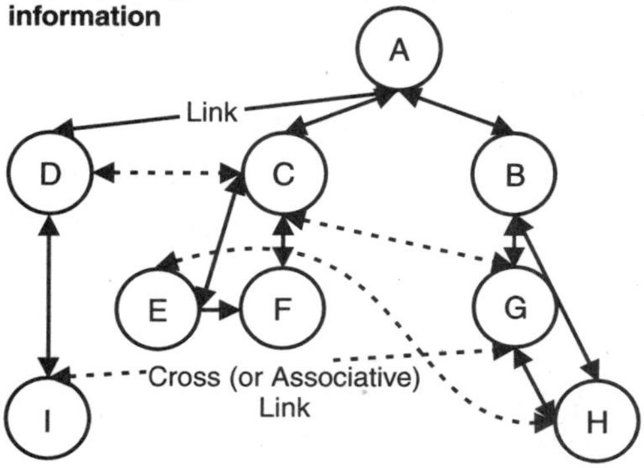

Figure 5 Web structure of information

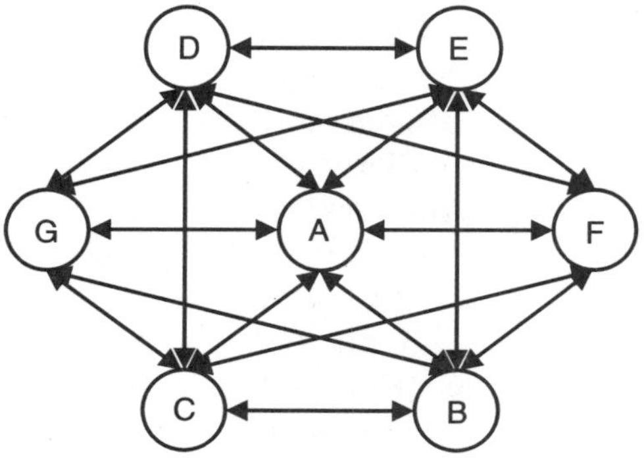

FIGURE 2.1   What is hypermedia?

Hypermedia, incidentally, is the platform of the World Wide Web—just one indication that hypertext is the text of the future. It will certainly continue to complement, and perhaps come to supplant, the book, much as the book supplanted the medieval codex, and codices replaced papyrus scrolls (Bolter 1991). To students who doubt this, we ask if they have seen any medieval codices lying about.

In our classroom, we used HyperCard on Macintosh computers. By the time this book comes out, HyperCard 3.0 should be available, which is a program designed to work on both Mac and Windows platforms. Although many other hypermedia authoring programs are available, and we know many teachers who are aficionados of other programs, such as HyperStudio or Digital Chisel, we think HyperCard is the best program for teachers. It is easy to learn and use, plus it has a wide variety of sophisticated design features and offers students options and modifications that other programs do not.

One of the primary selling points for HyperCard is its ease of use. Apple's selling site offers a web page on HyperCard for educators (http://hypercard.apple.com/success/story2.html). This site demonstrates how teachers and students can become proficient at the program in a few weeks. This leads to teacher confidence, concrete successes, administrative support, and the student design of interesting projects.

Why Hypermedia?

We believe that to be literate in the twenty-first century, students must become composers and readers of hypermedia. They must understand its possibilities, uses, and design. Since our future texts, even more so than our current ones, will be hypertextual, students will need to understand the conventions and construction of such texts.

Even more important, we have found that the use of hypermedia-based projects helps students to develop foundational learning competencies. Although the tool of hypermedia is itself an important one for making meaning, what is even more important is how the tool will be used to help students develop skills and construct meaning.

Hypermedia is currently being used in some schools as electronic worksheets for students to fill out. Such an instructionist (or information-transmission) application of hypermedia does not fulfill its promise for helping students to develop a twenty-first-century literacy, which we define as generating and representing information in multimedia form, becoming engaged with and organizing this information, and applying this information for multiple uses. As hypermedia guru Richard Lehrer told us, the promise of hypermedia as a means for students to compose and represent students' emerging understandings is untapped.

As we studied our classrooms as teacher-researchers, we found that the creation of hypermedia projects encourages students to develop many important foundational competencies and procedural understandings. The data, artifacts, and anecdotes we've collected from students indicate that the important features of hypertext encourage and support students to read, write, learn, and represent their understandings in new and more competent ways. Although we'll explore how these abilities are supported and demonstrated throughout our book, it's worth pointing out some of the most important ones here:

- *Role construction.* Students became active learners and decision makers as they composed hypermedia, and many previously reluctant students indicated that they came to name themselves as readers, writers, researchers, and learners as they pursued their projects. Many also indicated that they reconceived their roles as readers, writers, and learners as more complex, active, and participatory.

- *Idea development.* Responding to the challenge to fill computer screens with coherent and pointed sets of information, students were helped to identify topics, subtopics, key details, and supporting details. They came to understand the relationships of these kinds of information and the different work each could be asked to do. They also came to understand when a topic was too general, too specific, or off the point.

- *Classifying.* Our seventh graders became more adept at "chunking" information based on similarities, at differentiating data sets, and at seeing relationships among data.

- *Linking and organizing.* As they created planning webs and buttons, students were supported in understanding and using different ways of organizing and relating information. Their understanding of overall issues of text coherence was encouraged.

- *Representing understandings.* As might be expected, students became more aware of how different media work, and more savvy about what kind of media and combinations of media to use to communicate particular ideas. More surprising to us, the use of various media supported more developed writing on the part of many reluctant students.

■ *Developing and applying critical standards.* Students exhibited independent facility at articulating what makes various kinds of texts "good" and at applying these standards to their own work. This was closely related to our findings for revision.

■ *Sense of audience.* Hypermedia documents are visual and engaging, and they beg for an audience. Composing their own stacks and providing them to various readers helped our students to understand the purposes audiences want to fulfill as they read and helped them to understand where communication works and breaks down.

■ *Revision.* Related to the issues of audience and critical standards, we found that as different groups read and responded to a group's hyperstack, students were motivated and guided to revise their stacks as they responded to the comments and needs of their readers. Our data indicate that their revision was much deeper, thorough, and responsive when composing with hypermedia than it was when composing with paper and pencil.

■ *Collaboration.* Students were coached to consider how tasks could be decomposed and work divided. They were also asked to reflect on what helped groups to work well together and how to solve group problems. Surveys indicated that students valued group work more, felt they were better at group work, and knew more about how to help others participate in group work after the completion of their projects. The projects we describe provided the opportunities for a variety of both individual and group work.

Benefits of Integrated Inquiry Curricula

We believe that knowledge must be created in real situations, that it should be put to use, and that it is integrated. When we solve real-world problems, we don't ask what part is math, what science, and what language and divide up the task on those terms. We get after our problem holistically, bringing language and math and conceptual knowledge to bear whenever they are needed.

There are many planning frameworks and approaches to this kind of integrated inquiry curricula (Beane 1990; Brazee and Capelluti 1995; Clark 1997; Wood 1997, just to name a few). The variety of approaches signifies widespread agreement that integrating content-area learning helps students to make connections across knowledge domains. Procedural skills, conceptual understandings, and values have been shown to be most effectively taught and evaluated in meaningful, integrated contexts (Perkins 1986). Students who learn in integrated inquiry situations are afforded a plethora of advantages because this kind of curriculum:

- Addresses the demands of increasingly crowded curricula.
- Provides students greater ownership, agency, and control over their learning.
- Builds on students' prior knowledge and experience.
- Makes the purposes of learning clear from the start.
- Links learning and social action.
- Provides choices and opportunities.
- Increases motivation by connecting activities and purposes to students' need for relevance.
- Directly involves students in finding and creating information.
- Challenges learners to develop real-world thinking skills and reach for big understandings (Siu-Runyan and Faircloth 1995).
- Develops skills that can be adapted and used in various ways and develops ways of learning, problem solving, and knowing.
- Helps students to see connections between knowledge domains.
- Assists students to come to understand their own processes of learning.
- Provides functional contexts for learning that are clearly connected to the real world.
- Encourages students to bring their learning forward from one experience to the next.
- Widens students' meaning-making repertoires by allowing for various learning styles and asking students to extend and grow from their strengths to develop a range of learning strategies.
- Provides structures and real contexts for teaching and assessing outcomes in various knowledge domains and skill areas.
- Restructures the use of time in school so that the schedule makes more sense and is built around problem-solving activities and projects.
- Encourages team teaching and the use of community resources.

Curricular Trends

Middle school theorist James Beane (1990) has long advocated a student-centered, problem-cored, and inquiry-driven curriculum in which students learn about personally relevant and socially significant issues. He has argued that information in and of itself is too fleeting to be of any real use to students. What is important is that students learn how to learn, and they can achieve this with any kind of significant content that interests them. This goal is reached if teachers work to help students develop skills of critical thinking and learning as they engage with and use this content.

We want learning in our classrooms to be action oriented, contextualized, and purposeful (Perkins 1986). The reason is that learning requires motivation and the engagement of student interests and passions. Our own students showed insatiable passion for their own popular culture, for actually doing and making things that they believed were significant, and for using computers. Being effective teachers meant that we had to tap into these passions, to use them in conjunction with instruction and joint learning projects that would help students to grow beyond their current selves and develop an ever-widening repertoire of learning strategies.

This kind of thematic and project-oriented learning is not solely a middle school phenomenon. Many high schools are beginning to make use of this kind of curriculum too. In fact, such approaches are endorsed by the recent National Association of Secondary School Principals (NASSP) report, *Breaking Ranks* (1996).

One other important issue not to overlook is the importance of fun. When students are engaged in creating learning performances that are significant to them, they enjoy and become highly engaged in the flow of learning, and achieve more powerful kinds of learning (Csikszentmihalyi 1990).

Does the Shoe Fit? Hypermedia, Integration, and Inquiry

In our own school, we both had subject-area curricula that we were to cover each year. At the same time, because our school was making the transition from a junior high to a middle school, we were encouraged to do some team teaching and create some thematic integrated units. And then we had our own evolving views of how students learn best to add to the mix.

The balancing of our own purposes and beliefs with those of the school was and remains a political issue for us. Informed generally by the school curriculum, and more particularly by our own desire to help students become more wide-awake, humane, and independent learners, we developed an integrated curriculum that we hope has served both of these purposes and the students' own desire for significance.

The shape of our interdisciplinary curriculum began with a study of the self: Who Am I? It included a study of the various codes we use to communicate and present ourselves to the world. This unit culminated in the design of a personality profile hyperstack (see Chapter 4). We then proceeded through general thematic units on Ways of Thinking, Believing, and Being (with a unit on psychology), The Cultures of the World (anthropology and cultural studies), and How We Live Together (social issues and civil rights).

Over the course of several years, we devised major projects to be completed in conjunction with each unit. (Chapter 4 describes the first two projects; Chapters 5 through 8 explore the progress of our major hypermedia project during our cultural journalism unit; and the projects in our final unit will be noted in Chapter 9.)

These unit themes generated other themes of significant interest to the students. As a group of learners, we explored beliefs about kinship, legitimate sources of authority and community purpose, gender roles, the meaning of politics, history, the future. We asked how individuals and communities define law, truth, intelligence, education, roles, courtship, education, manners, parent-child relationships, priorities, the importance of arts, sports, rights, expression, and history. We looked at why customs exist and what they mean. In short, we studied whatever was of the most current importance about ourselves and our world, and we trusted that by developing their own purposes for learning, the skills of inquiry, and the confidence of learners, our students were setting out on life-long journeys to explore other issues that our inimitably interesting world will always have to offer.

After the End

One of the best things about the completed projects was that students wanted to present them to peers, parents, and the community. Our open house was one of several opportunities that they had to do so each year. Another virtue was that the students knew that the project could always be revised and improved, which made this unlike many other projects they had completed for school.

As we surveyed the computer lab during the open house, we saw two women from the senior citizens' home taking Mike's group's interactive quiz. They laughed with delight at the sound effects as the boys beamed behind them. Tina was helping an elderly gentleman who said he had never worked on a computer before, to add a card to her group's stack. He had some information from his service in World War II that they agreed would be useful to add to her stack on Hawaii. And Adam was busily correcting and adding some examples to a card his mother hadn't completely understood.

Parents, friends, people from the community, and school board members milled about, talking to our students and viewing stacks. Attendance of our students at this after-school activity was nearly 100 percent. They eagerly presented their stacks and watched their visitors browse through them. The principal and superintendent looked happy. The kids looked really happy too. Kids happy in school? Even though they were staying after school? That's really saying something!

How we got to this relatively happy place is what the rest of this book is about.

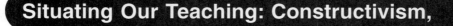

Chapter 3

Situating Our Teaching: Constructivism,

Cognitive Apprenticeship, and

Student Design

Important Points

This chapter explains how a clearly articulated theory of learning can help guide teaching. We explain our own theory and the teaching frameworks that guided the practice described in this book. *Some readers might want to read the later chapters that describe actual practice before returning to this chapter to become familiar with the theories underlying that practice.*

➡ All teaching is informed by theories and beliefs, though these are often implicitly held. The most "wide-awake" (Greene 1978) and flexible instruction is informed by research-based theories about how people learn. The projects described in this book are framed by theories and research regarding constructivism, and the teaching frameworks of cognitive apprenticeship and student-designed learning.

➡ Constructivism is a theory of knowledge that all understanding is personally created based on the learner's experience and interactions with the world.

➡ Cognitive apprenticeship is a teaching framework that structures and supports the learning of target skills used in functional and social contexts.

➡ Student design is a framework that organizes student work around a complex of procedural skills that are ways of learning and knowing, such as questioning, finding information, and organizing data.

I feel like I have been struggling my whole career to figure out how to give kids ownership of their learning at the same time that I retain an important role as a teacher who supports and guides and assists them. I mean, it's my job to help them know and do things that they can't achieve on their own. So much of this natural learning stuff seems soft and flouncy to me. Like "anything goes" or "catch the wave!" Where's the teaching? Where's the answerability of the kids to reach justifiable conclusions and do ever more competent work? How can I as a teacher actually prove the kids have learned something of value? On the other hand, this teaching with cognitive apprenticeship and student design finally feels right to me. The kids are doing work that is meaningful to them, I am teaching them how to do that work, and I can name and demonstrate what they are learning.

　　Jeff, from his teaching journal, February 1994

We're teaching kids how to do things, and they are learning really important content on their own terms. This kind of teaching has a sharp edge on it—the kids are loving it. Who am I fooling? I'm loving it too!

　　Paul, hallway conversation, February 1994

Following is an audiotape transcript from February 1994. A group studying Iceland is taking a first pass at organizing the data they have collected about their research question: What would a traveler need to know and do to enjoy a trip to Iceland?

T: I don't get this.

J: How are we . . .?

B: What are we supposed to do with all this stuff [reference to notes, books, references, and printouts they had collected]?

T: We're supposed to organize it.

C: Yeah, but how? There's so much of it.

T: We can't use all this.

J: That's the point. We have to pick stuff we can use.

B: Put stuff together that goes together.

T: I still don't get this.

J: Chunk it, you know, like he said. Or we'll never know what stuff to put together when we write.

B: Are there things that seem to go together? If we can put some ideas in groups, like possible answers to the question, we could name the groups and organize how it would go with an issue tree or something.

C: Er, what could we name the groups of stuff?

J: Mmm. Like things to do in Iceland? Things to see?

C: Write that down!

This group of boys had previously learned how to use various organizational tools and are now attempting to use the tools on their own with their own set of collected data. How were they brought to this point? How well were they doing? Should we have intervened as teachers to give them more support?

"Wide-Awake" Teaching: Theories that Guide Us

Our personal theories and beliefs about learning affect everything that we as teachers have done and do in the classroom, what we feel uncomfortable with and critique about our teaching, how we have tried and still try to improve what we do with our students.

Educational researchers have documented how teachers' implicit, internal beliefs about student learning and thinking affect how they teach in the classroom (Bruer 1993) and how articulating and attempting to implement instruction consistent with beliefs helps teachers to teach more powerfully (Greene 1978).

We use two major guides to our teaching—the theory of constructivism, about the nature of knowledge itself, and our instructional frameworks for implementing constructivist principles in the classroom: cognitive apprenticeship and student design.

Constructivism

A major problem in education is that students perceive their environment (curricula, textbooks, computer programs, tasks, and teachers) in ways that may be different from that intended by teachers (von Glasersfeld 1996). Educational researchers tell us that this is because each student actively and internally constructs his own representations of things;

learning is a constructive activity that students themselves must carry out. This insight is at the center of the theory known as constructivism (Julyan and Duckworth 1996; von Glasersfeld 1996). What this means is that teachers cannot simply transfer knowledge and concepts directly from their "head" into the "student's head." Rather, students must construct their own knowledge, concepts, and meaning from instruction, learning environments, and experience.

Constructivism is a theory about the nature of knowledge, and thus it is important for all teachers to consider because it affects how all of us think and learn. Based on the work of Piaget, Vygotsky, and others, constructivism is beginning to have a major impact on the goals teachers set, instructional strategies, and methods of assessment (Fosnot 1996).

The purpose of knowledge is not to produce a representation of some independent reality that will be the same across all students; rather, knowledge is constructed by each individual as he tries to impose meaning on and make sense out of his world and his experiences (von Glasersfeld 1996). This does not mean that we will disagree about everything or that we should allow students to hold naive misconceptions about a subject, but it does mean that it is up to each student to create meaning from his experiences in a classroom and to think on his own. It is, after all, his own knowledge.

According to Gould (1996), classrooms that encourage the active construction of meaning focus on big understandings and powerful ideas rather than facts, and they encourage students to ask their own questions, follow their own interests, make their own connections, reformulate ideas, and reach unique conclusions. Students and teachers are aware that the world is a complex place in which multiple perspectives exist and that truth is often a matter of interpretation, or exists in the conversation between various perspectives.

The theory of constructivism challenges teachers to create innovative learning environments where students are encouraged to think and explore. Learners must play an active role in selecting and defining activities that are challenging and intrinsically motivating to them. Most important, there must be appropriate teacher support as learners build concepts, schemata, cognitive skills, and problem-solving abilities. It is also important for teachers to guide students to develop and apply critical standards for what they know—to make their reasoning visible and the knowledge they have constructed accountable and justifiable.

Constructivism means that the purpose of lessons has changed from years ago, when teachers were expected to provide clear, detailed explanations of subject matter, dispensing knowledge to students who would "get it" if they explained it in a clear, organized manner or in multiple modes of presentation. Instead, constructivism suggests a new purpose for class work: to encourage students to construct their own full understandings of the workings of a subject area. Constructing an understanding requires that students have opportunities to articulate their ideas, test those ideas through experimentation and conversation, and consider connections between the phenomena they are examining and other aspects of their lives (Julyan and Duckworth 1996). For example, to "do" math is to conjecture: to invent and extend ideas about mathematical objects, to test, debate, and revise or replace those ideas (Shifter 1996).

These new perspectives on the learning process have provided a drastically revised picture of what should be taking place in classrooms (Shifter 1996). In many quarters, teaching is being reconceived as the provision of activities designed to encourage and facilitate the constructive process. The constructivist classroom is meant to become a community of inquiry, a problem-posing and problem-solving environment in which developing an approach to thinking about concepts and issues is valued more highly than memorizing algorithms and using them to get the right answers on tests (Brown and Campione 1994; Cognition and Technology Group at Vanderbilt 1994; Erickson 1997; Shifter 1996).

Our work is an attempt to build such a community of inquiry in the classroom. (You will see how the theory of constructivism drives much of what we do with hypermedia.) To aid students' construction of reading and social studies, we ask our students to articulate what they know, defend how they know it, discuss it with others, critique it, debate it, and revise.

We ask the students to articulate their critical standards—their beliefs for what makes something of quality (e.g., a "good" research question is one that does not have a yes-no answer, is of interest to peers, and can sustain research over a period of time). Students negotiate standards of quality (what makes a "good" hypermedia document, a good question, a good organization for one's information). And these critical standards evolve to higher standards over time. (For more on critical standards, see Erickson and Lehrer, in press.)

Cognitive Apprenticeship

Consistent with constructivism is a method of instruction, cognitive apprenticeship, that specifies how the learning environment should be structured and why. Collins, Brown, and Newman (1989) explain that before schools appeared, apprenticeship was the most common means of learning knowledge and skills required for expert practice in fields ranging from tailoring to sculpting to medicine and law. There are many differences between formal schooling and apprenticeship, but the most important is that in schools, skills and knowledge have become detached and abstracted from their uses in the real world—a problem that cognitive apprenticeship tries to remedy.

In apprenticeship learning, the target skills are continually used in their social and functional contexts (Collins et al. 1989). Teaching is not didactic. Rather, apprentices learn knowledge and skills through "observation, coaching, and successive approximation." This means that learners observe the targeted skills in the context of using them and while seeing a range of skill levels and strategies for accomplishing the skills. After observing the skills being used, learners practice the skills while others coach them, and little by little they refine the skills until they gain expertise.

The movement to bring cognitive apprenticeship into the classrooms to help solve some of the problems of schooling is consistent with constructivism. The "cognitive" part is that the target skills are no longer things like tailoring, painting, or other physical skills; instead, the skills are cognitive, like finding and organizing information or evaluating and reflecting.

We have come to conceive of learning as being apprenticed into new understandings and more powerful ways of doing things, and of teaching as "assisted performance" (Tharp and Gallimore 1990). This model of learning owes a lot to the Russian psychologist Lev Vygotsky, who argued that children can always do more with assistance (whether provided by adults or peers) than they can do alone. He felt that all teaching should take place in this zone of proximal development (ZPD), which is that zone just beyond what students can do independently but can achieve with help.

In this book, we show both why and how we used technology to design a fruitful learning environment in the classroom, an environment that is consistent with both constructivism and cognitive apprenticeship. In our classroom, students don't just produce or construct anything they like of any kind of quality. Rather, knowledge must be accountable, and the means of knowing must be made visible so that students can observe the cognitive skills in the context of their use (Lehrer 1993; Mercer 1995). In other words, students must learn how to learn new things, they must learn procedures and concepts that are valid and applicable in the world, and they must be able to defend how they know what they know.

We worked very hard to make mental processes explicit and visible, and to structure and sequence the learning activities in such a way that students would attain new conceptual and procedural understandings. We provided the instructional support that helped students gain cognitive skills as they designed their multimedia documents. This approach does not preclude students' making their own choices and directing their own learning. It does, however, create structures and parameters within which this will occur. For instance, you will read how our own students asked personally relevant research questions. However, they did so by using instructional structures that helped them to ask powerful questions and to reflect on how to do so most fruitfully. This is teaching and learning with the kind of edge we had been looking for and is consistent with our beliefs about knowledge and learning.

Hypermedia, Apprenticeship, and Design

We wanted students' thinking to be supported and stretched in a social context in which they were involved in problem-solving activities with peers (Rogoff 1990). Cognitive apprenticeship provided one instructional method to support this thinking. We also needed a concrete tool and a teaching framework for implementing this method in the classroom. Hypermedia was one concrete tool that would help us to develop students' literacy skills, and student design was the framework.

As we began to redefine our teaching as "assisting performances" (Tharp and Gallimore 1990) rather than donating information to students, we came to see our job as helping them to achieve new learning "performances" as they prepared and implemented action plans or created documents and artifacts of significance to them. In these contexts, we would provide instruction and guidance to help them push beyond their current boundaries of ability and understanding. As Vygotsky (1978) reminds us, the teacher's job is to help students perform and understand what they cannot perform or understand on their own.

To organize our instruction and help us implement our new view of teaching, we used the notion of student-design learning. This framework works to make task demands and student thinking visible, so that as teachers we can intervene and assist in ever more competent performances of learning in which real work is done and useful artifacts are created.

The Notion of Student Design

Based on Dewey's (1910) notion that education should be about the structuring of learning experiences, Perkins (1986) suggests that students should design knowledge. Although he doesn't limit this notion of design to particular subjects or problems, we used his metaphor to undergird instruction leading to student-designed documents on hypermedia and video. The notion of design and its particular uses with technology-based education were introduced to us by Richard Lehrer of the University of Wisconsin. He met with us several times as we planned and implemented this model, and his graduate student, Julie Erickson, was a continual presence in our school over several years when we initiated and revised our design projects with our students. Both believe that hypermedia possesses special potential for extending students' current abilities, helping them to outgrow their current selves.

To guide our work with hypermedia, we used a framework that Rich developed that specifies cognitive skills children use in designing with hypermedia (Lehrer 1993; Lehrer, Erickson, and Connell 1994):

Planning

- Defining the nature of the problem
- Asking questions of interest
- Managing the project (assign tasks, roles, develop time line)

Transforming

- Finding information
- Documenting search techniques (cite sources)
- Developing new information (interview questionnaire)
- Selecting information (take notes, summarize)
- Organizing information (outline, pyramids, issue tree)
- Representing information (combine sound, graphics, text, and animation to express ideas effectively)

Evaluating

- Evaluating the design (critique others, provide feedback to peers)
- Public speaking (present hypermedia screens or document for critique)
- Self-evaluation (evaluate own hypermedia stack)

Revising

- Soliciting peer feedback

- Reflecting on document as a whole (did it accomplish its intended purpose?)
- Revising the design

These are the four primary cognitive processes students use when composing with hypermedia. These processes parallel those involved in written composition (Hayes and Flower 1980) and extend to electronic composition, such as providing multiple organizational structures and media representations for the audience (Lehrer 1993). In this way, hypermedia composition supports traditional composition *and* looks to the future by broadening our current notion of text and textual composing to include programming, visual images, movement, video, and the composition of other kinds of meaning-laden texts (Smagorinsky and Coppock 1994; Wilhelm 1997).

The hypermedia platform encourages connections and representations of meaning that will become part of the learner's repertoire for seeing and thinking about the world. Using this hypermedia framework, we could help our students to become designers—designers of hypermedia documents in one respect, but, really, designers of knowledge. Design is concerned with the interplay of purpose and structure in the context of student activity. This is played out in a concern with authenticity, extensibility of knowledge, and the actual use of artifacts that are created with this knowledge.

DiSessa (1992) claims that encouraging children to become designers (e.g., with hypermedia) will prove profitable for several reasons. First, designing a physical artifact presents many opportunities to support productive activities that are not always seen in the classroom—activities like reflection and revision. The activity of students' constructing something also provides multiple occasions for them to cooperate—environments where individuals with different skills and interests can participate effectively. Students have the opportunity to share ideas about the products and how they designed them; they learn about multiple viewpoints for examining both the products and the process of design.

Second, design is an activity within the ordinary range of interests, goals, and skills of children. Design environments provide opportunities for students with different skills to participate and contribute. Developing a product can also generate student interest through the personal ownership and pride that comes with building something.

Third, design provides an overriding goal that can provide continuity over a sustained period of time. The goal of constructing something continues to orient class discussions, and it provides continuity to all activities, from planning to product development to evaluation and revision.

Finally, constructing something that has a purpose, like designing software to teach younger children about fractions (Harel 1991), contributes an element of authenticity to the task. It provides the motivation, criteria, and justification for students to critique and improve the construction. Thus, when students examine the purpose of their design, this naturally suggests criteria for evaluation of the product. Moreover, there is no one way to design, no correct answer—only better or worse designs for serving a particular purpose.

Traditional projects, for instance, are often displayed somewhere in the school but are rarely used by anyone, and even more rarely used by subsequent students as something to build on and extend (Lehrer, Erickson, and Connell 1994). Yet professional communities of practice and design in the arts, sciences, and business constantly build on and revise others' work and models in incremental steps.

In our classroom, we collaborated with students to create design documents for tutoring others (documents placed in our school media center and local library to serve as learning aids for the public), serving social purposes (advising travelers and business interests), and communicating (exchanging documents with learning buddies and partner schools) in ways that structured information in usable ways. Knowledge, after all, is distinguished from information by its structure (Perkins 1991), extensibility, systematicity, and applicability.

The design framework was powerful for us and our students because it framed instruction in terms of student needs and purposes (our students always chose their own groups, their own topics, and their own research questions) and because it served as a model for integrating curriculum. The framework is specific about what students must do to become designers of knowledge, in contrast to most other instructional models, which are typically quite vague and "underspecified."

Without Sorcery: Researcher's Apprentices

Here is a transcript of an initial roundtable session for research questions. The students had compiled their list of possible questions about a stack on traveling to Italy and were beginning to present and critique the questions.

C: These aren't very good.

Teacher: No, no, no. It's a good start. I like this one about if most people speak English. Mmmm. That seems important to me. And it would make a difference to how you prepare for your trip. And this one—What's the economy of Italy? What do you mean? Who would care about that? What difference does the answer make?

B: Well, you have to know about money and stuff.

Teacher: Is that what the question asks? Check out the help sheet we made on questioning to help you out. I'll be back in a bit. *(Teacher moves to another group.)*

A: *(looking at help sheet)* Bogus! We're supposed to make sure the question is interesting to us and other people. That economy thing doesn't grab me at all.

C: It's one of the cultural institutions. But why should we give a care?

B: Let's change it.

A: How?

B: What do you need to know about money [to get around Italy]?

C: Italian money? Buying stuff with Italian money?

A: How much is it worth in American money?

B: *(writing note)* Yeah. What do you need to know about Italian money . . .

In this excerpt, we see multiple levels of assistance being provided. The roundtable session for presenting and critiquing the questions is a way in which the instructional environment focuses and assists the students. The help sheet, devised during previous instructional activities, also helps guide the work. The teacher assists, peers help each other, and students use what they have learned to assist themselves. Through the multiple forms of assistance, the students are being apprenticed as inquirers who are learning how to ask powerful, interesting, and answerable research questions.

Unlike the situation of Disney's Sorcerer's Apprentice, who is controlled by the tool he uses, the students here are helped to do work that is focused and fits their own purposes. They are consolidating what they have learned and using those skills to do new work. Through the assistance, they exercise a measure of control over the process—all without the help of a magic broom! The process of real researchers is made clear to them as they engage in the process. No tricks. No magic. No sorcery. Just informed teaching that can lead to some solid student work.

Chapter 4

Setting It Up: Getting Kids into the Flow

of Hypermedia Design

Important Points

This chapter begins describing our classroom practice. We explain how to start with short projects that can potentially lead to longer ones. Paper and pen projects from previous years can easily be translated to hypercard form. We also discuss sequencing both within and between units, because one project can build skills, experience, and motivation for approaching the next project, which will be more challenging and sophisticated. This sequencing of projects can supplement traditional curricula or become an integrated, inquiry-based curriculum of thematic units focused on students' designing projects to answer their own questions. The following chapters examine the process of helping students to develop specific target skills important to constructing knowledge across the curriculum.

➤ Students need to be prepared and "apprenticed" into the skills of knowledge design and hypermedia use. Some knowledge design skills are general, but many skills and demands will be specific to the topic and the task.

➤ Assignments within a project need to be carefully sequenced as students see models, use models, receive assistance as they learn, and are brought to the point where they independently use cognitive skills. Throughout this process, students are guided and helped to achieve new skills through the assistance of teachers, peers, and self-regulated assistance. Teaching in this framework focuses on helping students develop procedural skills. A series of projects can also be sequenced so that new skills are introduced, and older skills fine-tuned and developed over time.

➤ A design curriculum takes time. It can, however, be the whole curriculum and can work to address all of the conceptual and procedural goals of traditional curricula. And a design curriculum can do so more effectively.

➤ Completing a series of projects can help students understand and internalize the framework and skills of design so that these skills can be used independently.

Some of the other students seem to know what they want to write before they write it. Like they can see it in their heads or something. But I see pictures of what I'm thinking, not words. So when I could draw, or scan something that I'd made into the computer, then that really helped me to write. It showed me what I wanted to write about.

Cassie, seventh grader

At the beginning of the year, I didn't even know how to turn on the computer. But now I can make a stack—no sweat. I can start with my own question, find out about it, and put it all together into a really excellent hyperstack. And no sweat!

Jordan, end of seventh grade

To get started with your own hypermedia project, we suggest starting with a short, easily containable project. In fact, throughout our various projects with hypermedia and video, most of the students' work was done off the computer or camera. Using the technology informed our work throughout the unit, but was never actually used until much of the significant work had already been done. For this reason, it is easy to take a project or writing assignment that you already do in class and translate it to hypermedia.

This is how we got started. We decided that once our students were done with a personality profile project, we would help them to translate it to hypermedia. What happened is that many of the problems with our unit and the supposedly completed profiles were rectified through the joint community learning experience that we created and that was in fact invited by the platform of hypermedia.

This small-scale and fairly simple project led over the years to ever more complex, challenging, and longer projects.

Personality Profile Assignment

 Seven years ago now, when Paul and I first began to team-teach, our seventh-grade students ended their first quarter of study by composing personality profiles. A personality profile is a piece of writing that helps us to get to know a person by describing—or profiling—the subject's personality, favorite activities, traits, and the like. The feature section of the newspaper often runs personality profiles, and magazines like *People* are filled with them.

I asked students to write profiles of themselves, which we subsequently published in a classroom anthology. The assignment was successful because adolescent students are intensely self-interested and are engaged in defining themselves to themselves and to their peers. The assignment fit their developmental needs, particularly as it helped students from six different elementary schools to introduce themselves to each other. The assignment was a good way to start the year for two other reasons: I knew the students would have something to write about, and it helped me get to know them as people and as students.

We began the profile unit by reading three student models of personality profiles, composed in previous years, and ranking them from most successful to least successful. Then we defined what a personality profile was and listed what would need to be done and included to make a profile an interesting and satisfying piece to read. From this student-generated list, we came up with a criteria checksheet to guide our writing. This kind of rubric or checksheet was a tool that we used in all of our projects to help students articulate and apply their evolving conceptions of quality. The resulting criteria list was an assessment tool for us as teachers because the students made their thinking visible. We would then know how they perceived a task and what needed to be done to achieve a quality product. It also worked for the students by making class standards explicit. Since they made the standards, they owned them, renegotiated them as the unit progressed, and worked to meet the standards they had agreed on.

The criteria that one class agreed on were fairly typical:

- *Hook.* You need an exciting story or insight to start off.
- *Physical description.* Show what the person looks like—hair, body, face, eyes.
- *Clothes.* Show what the person wears, including brand names, styles, and colors
- *Favorite places.* Show the details of the person's room at home or a place they like to hang out. Include decorations, furniture, lighting, colors, etc.
- *Tastes.* Show the person's taste in music, food, books, and any other likes or dislikes.
- *Activity.* Show the person doing something they like to do.
- *Quotes.* Have some quotes that the person really said that show what they are like.

- *Quotes from friends.* Have some exact words from friends describing the person.
- *Make sure you show the person.* Don't tell about them.

Profile Problems

After students read student models, defined the task and articulated standards, and read some professional profiles of interest to them, they were assigned to write a first draft of a profile about themselves. And although the assignment was generally successful, the problems did always seem to start piling up.

Cassie demonstrated a fairly typical problem of writer's block. Cassie, a quiet but fairly conscientious girl, wanted to do well but found it difficult to get started with her writing. And when she did get something down, she found it hard to know where to go next. When she got frustrated enough, she would quit, and that sometimes didn't come to my attention until considerable time and energy had been wasted.

Since our first personality profile criterion was to have an exciting story about ourselves (or "hook") to start the paper, Cassie struggled with what to write to begin her profile. Even after extensive brainstorming, she was still stumped. "You must have an interesting hobby or experience that would make people sit up and take notice," I urged her.

Cassie eventually wrote a beautiful hook about a ride with her brother on a roller coaster. But she was then stumped about what to do next.

Jordan was representative of many disengaged and LD-labeled students. He expressed confusion about assignments and usually seemed to do the minimum. He professed, "I hate writing," and the first draft of his profile was excellent evidence for this assertion. His paper was a list of telegraphic facts. "My name is Jordan," he started, then listed his sporting interests with statements like, "I play hockey." He wrote a few details about his sister, said he loved his family, and concluded, "I play on the Might Mites team. My sister is a freshman. She figure skates. We went on a trip this summer. The End!"

Jordan was typical of many other seventh graders in that the ideas in his profile were anemically underdeveloped and organized as a list. He related some facts but without any sense of purpose or rhetorical awareness.

I asked him why he didn't put the information about his sister with the information about his family, and why he split the information about playing hockey and the name of his hockey team. He explained, "We're supposed to include our feelings so I just did that. Then I remembered that I hate people always putting down hockey . . ." His organization reflected personal associations that would not be clear to a typical reader.

Jordan's paper was also typical in that he mentioned many potentially interesting ideas that he failed to pursue and fill out with specific examples or anecdotes. Despite our discussion, his second draft showed little improvement.

Finally, there was Mark, a good student who typically generated too much material. He included many tangential details in his profile and went off in wild directions that had little to do with the topic of his own personality. Although much of what he composed was well written, as a whole it was fragmented, disorganized, and overly long. He bridled somewhat at his peer group's suggestions for improvement with the retort, "I worked *really* hard on this!" He told me that he deserved an A because "I put a lot of effort into this," and said his peer group was at fault for not "getting it. It makes perfect sense to me."

These three students typified many of my major concerns about student writers: problems finding, generating, and representing information; problems with motivation and engagement; problems organizing the material; and problems considering audience.

A Year of Hypermedia

The personality profile was part of an integrated unit in language arts and social studies that focused on identity and personality. We called the unit "Who Am I?" During the summer, we had discussed pursuing a major project using hypermedia. We thought the profile project would be a good time to introduce this software platform to our students so that they would be familiar with it for later work.

We were given hypermedia tutoring by two eighth-grade students who helped us understand how to create a *template*—a set of blank cards that students could fill out and link. Each criterion that our students articulated became the topic for a card; there was a card for physical description, for a favorite setting, tastes and habits, and so on. (See Figure 4.1.)

We brainstormed together for a visual, aural, or graphic exhibit that could be included on each card that would in some way complement the written information about the topic.

I then created a stack of cards for students to fill out and connect

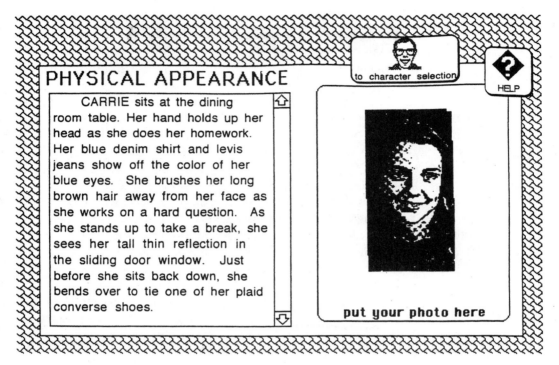

FIGURE 4.1   Personality profile stack cards.

through the creation of buttons and links to other cards. Finally, with the help of a savvy student, I created a Help button for each card that could provide instructions and examples on what is called a *pop-up field* (see Figure 4.2).

This seemed to be an excellent way to introduce students to the possibilities of hypermedia. A scaffolded stack of hypercards had been created for them but needed to be filled out. Students transferred their written papers to the hypercards; they were introduced to hypermedia tools, how to scan in photos, create pictures and graphics, record in sound, and create their own buttons to link networks of completed cards.

Assistance was provided to the students by the model of the template itself, the Help buttons on each card, models that were created and shared by classmates, and instructional help. The provision of multiple modes of teaching assistance by the environment, the teacher, and peers fit our notions of effective teaching. After this very guided work, students had de-

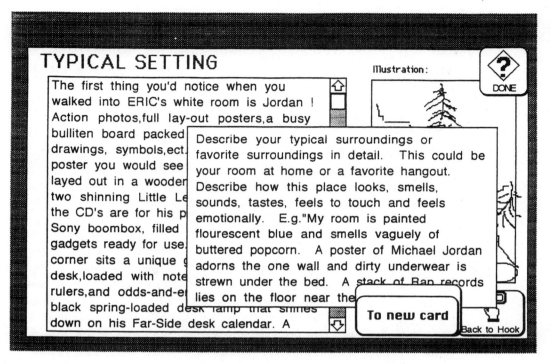

FIGURE 4.2   Mark's typical surroundings (personality profile stack).

veloped the expertise to create some new cards from scratch. They then linked these new cards to the existing stack.

Since hypermedia, like knowledge itself, is structured and extensible, we returned to this project later in the year and built on it with a new and more extended project. We created cards about literary characters, which the students connected to particular cards about themselves, thereby relating their lives to character lives. Through all of this, students began to build proficiency as designers of hypermedia. By the end of the year, these original stacks had been extended into highly developed networks that showed the connections, similarities, and differences between each student and a variety of literary characters, historical figures, and significant others.

One problem we often encounter when using computers is that students frequently face unfamiliar problems and need help to solve them— requiring lots of teacher energy and student downtime. In this assignment, if students hit on a problem regarding the content of a card, they had a Help button available to them. If they had a problem with a tool or procedure regarding hypermedia, we had taped help sheets for hypermedia tools near each computer and a scanning help sheet on the optical scanner. (See Figure 4.3.)

How Hypermedia Helped

I wrote in my journal that "the level of enthusiasm for the project, and for the writing itself, just jumped the moment students turned on the computer and began to learn how to use the hypercard program and its tools."

Jordan noticed that his short sentences did not fill the field on each hypercard screen. Interestingly, he fooled around with shrinking the fields, but felt that the shrunken field looked "stupid," so he expanded the fields to their original size and used the Help button to begin working on filling out the card. Jordan was enthused with scanning in photographs and drawing graphics. He became so enamored with putting in special backgrounds and special effects that we had to make a rule about completing required elements of each card before adding new elements. This proved to be a great motivation for Jordan, who visited the computer room after school for three days running so that he could complete the requirements of his stack and then work with some of hypermedia's special features.

Jordan was joined by many classmates. We found, during this project and throughout the subsequent years, that kids would often spend their free hour, lunch, and before- and after-school time in the lab, eager to work on their hypermedia documents. We don't want to minimize this problem, but it certainly is a happy one to have. (Our teaching team lobbied for a computer aide because of this traffic, and we eventually got one.)

Mark, on the other hand, experienced the opposite problem. Much of his material did not fit under any of the card topics, which taken together served as an outline of required information. When he created a new card for some of this material, he decided instead to delete the information, telling me that "this stuff really doesn't have anything to do with me [or my personality]." When I asked him what had helped him to realize this, he explained that it was "creating the buttons." When pressed for further explanation, he said, "There were no other cards that I could connect the new card to. Then I saw that the new card didn't fit the topic of my personality." The requirement to link cards to related cards forced Mark to

HyperCard Tools

Tool	Name	Action
🖑	Browse tool	selects button, edits fields (▤)
⬭	Button tool	used to create and change buttons *(See: objects)*
▤	Field tool	used to create and change fields *(see: Objects)*
⌞⌝	Selection tool	selects a rectangular area—including white space
⬭	Lasso tool	selects an irregular area—no white space
∂	Pencil	draws a line
🖌	Paintbrush	draws with selected pattern of specified brush shape
⬦	Eraser	erases graphics
＼	Straight Line	draws a straight line
🖍	Spray Can	sprays paint of pattern selected
▭	Rectangle	draws a rectangle with selected line width
▢	Rounded Rectangle	draws a rounded rectangle with selected line width
◯	Oval	draws an oval with selected line width
♡	Curve	draws a curve with selected line width
⬡	Regular Polygon	draws a regular polygon with selected line width
◿	Polygon	draws an irregular polygon with selected line width
⬦	Paint Bucket	fills the surrounded graphic with specified pattern
A	Paint Text	enters paint text

FIGURE 4.3 Examples of help sheets we used, such as hypertools, a scanner help sheet, and a design help sheet.

Scanning Pictures

1. Open Hyperscan 2.01 alias.
2. Put picture in upper left-hand corner of scanner.
3. Click on Preview.
4. Grab corner and position box around picture.
5. Click on Scan.
6. Don't adjust Auto Exposure.
7. Insert your disk.
8. Pull down Hyperscan menu and highlight Save Image To (and let go)
9. Click the Desktop button.
10. Double-click your disk on the screen.
11. Double-click your stack and the picture will be saved to a New Card in your stack.
12. Quit HyperCard.

At Your Station: Directions for Editing Pictures
1. Use the Selection tool to select part of pictures you want. Copy to a New Card.
2. Use the Selection tool then Go-Options Rotate (grab corner to flip right-side up).
3. Options Perspective lets you change size or shape.

FIGURE 4.3   continued

reflect on his topic and the connections in his writing. He realized the lack of connection that typified his own writing, which was a major breakthrough.

Cassie quickly completed her own stack and added one new card to her stack. She told me that composing was easier for her on hypercards: "I can always use the Help button for help. The cards [fields] are easier to write on than a big sheet of paper. You know you can do it. And I liked adding pictures." It turned out that Cassie was artistic, and she scanned in several of her own drawings to her hyperstack. The artwork seemed to motivate and scaffold much of her writing in that it visually illustrated her main points. This helped her know what to write and to communicate her main points.

She explained, "I knew how to describe myself with art, so when I scanned in my self-portrait, it was easier to do it in writing." Interestingly, she had not thought to write about her interest in artwork in her first two drafts. "It just seems so obvious to do it [write about her artwork] when you can show it to people."

Hypercard Help Sheet

Starting
1. Turn on computer.
2. Insert your disk.
3. Double-click your disk to open it.
4. Double-click your stack to open it.
5. Option-m to open the message box.
6. Type in - set userlevel to 5.
7. Press the return key.
8. Option-m to close the message box or click on the close box in the upper left corner.

Buttons
To make a button:
1. Click on the button tool.
2. Pull down Object menu and select New Button.
3. A button will appear on the screen. To work the button you must double-click the button itself.

To delete a button:
1. Click on the button tool.
2. Press the delete key.

To copy a button:
1. Click on the button tool.
2. Click on the button you want to copy.
3. Press Option-c to copy the button.
4. Use the arrow keys to go to the card you want to use the button on.
5. Press Option-v to paste the button.

Fields
To make a field, delete a field, or copy a field do the same operations described above for buttons except use the field tool.

To type in a field:
1. Click on the browse tool.
2. Click in the upper left corner of the field box and type.
3. To change the field operations double-click the field (Font, Scrolling, etc.)

To Make a New Card
Go to Edit and highlight New Card or press Option-n.

To Save
1. Pull down the field menu.
2. Select Save a Copy and release.
3. Change the name of the stack to what you want.
4. Check the screen to be sure you save to your disk and to the Macintosh hard drive by clicking the drive button.
5. Press Save.

To Quit
1. First save.
2. Quit HyperCard in file menu or Option-q.
3. Close your disk and hard drive.
4. Drag your disk to the trash can.
5. Go through computer shut down procedure.

Keyboard Equivalents
Option-c = copy
Option-n = new card
Option-p = print menu
Option-v = paste
Option-m = show message box
Option-q = quit HyperCard

FIGURE 4.3   continued

Computer Glitches: What We Wished We'd Known from the Start

There were a few problems with using hypermedia, and initially, some of these problems caused us great frustration. Being in the computer room reminded me of what my father had told me about having children: "It's the place where you'll experience your best and worst moments." Jeff wrote in his journal that "if it weren't for the students' great excitement I would probably trash the whole idea [of using hypermedia, not of having kids!]."

Scheduling the computer room was a problem. Often computers did not work; the program would freeze or do something that we simply didn't have the expertise to fix immediately. Although we would ask students to design a card on paper while we worked to fix the computer, valuable class time was lost. (See Figure 4.4.) We learned how to unlock disks and programs that students had locked. We learned that Open Apple B makes fields and buttons disappear. We learned that sometimes Userlevels need to be reset, and we learned how to do it. Each one of these lessons took place during class time and caused us frustration with computers and the project.

Our advice is for teachers to know HyperCard before starting a unit on it, to have a HyperCard book available while teaching, and to have another teacher or student who knows HyperCard (or whatever program you are using) available for the first few days of introducing the software to students. Also, we doubt if we would have continued our work with hypermedia if we had not known how the use of hypermedia and project-oriented curriculum fit our philosophy and theory regarding student learning (Erickson 1997; Lehrer 1993; Lehrer et al. 1994; also see Chapter 3).

In addition, although the HyperCard program itself automatically saves changes, lots of students lost their data or had their disks destroyed. Some disks were clearly destroyed on purpose, by students opening the disk physically and defacing it with a pencil. One student put his disk through the washing machine, stuck as it was in his back jeans pocket. Our advice is to be ready for this. In fact, be ready for anything. Students need to learn to protect and keep track of their disks. They need to learn to respect other people's property. They need to learn to back up important work on a hard drive or backup disk. (Perhaps with the advent of Iomega's Zip and Jaz Drives, every student will be able to carry around her own hard disk.) This is all part of living in the computer age.

Finally, most of the links students created during this first project were

Card Plan Sheet

Directions: Use this sheet to plan your individual cards. The information on the bottom should help to design and plan your cards.

Name _____
Hour _____
Culture _____
Group # _____

Card Name: _____

Background Info: _____
Graphic Info: _____
Sound Info: _____

Button Name: _____   Button Name: _____
   Icon: _____   Icon: _____
   Effect: _____   Effect: _____
   Link to: _____   Link to: _____
   Script: _____   Script: _____
Button Name: _____   Button Name: _____
   Icon: _____   Icon: _____
   Effect: _____   Effect: _____
   Link to: _____   Link to: _____
   Script: _____   Script: _____

Field: _____   "A" Tool Text: _____
Style: _____   Font: _____
Font: _____   Font Size: _____

FIGURE 4.4 An early card design sheet.

very simple. In effect, they had just transferred their paper to hypercards without making use of the multidimensional possibilities of hyperspace. We realized that hypermedia could help teach students how to represent, organize, manipulate, and present information, but that it would take time. This is a crucial point often unacknowledged in schools: *significant learning takes time.*

Toward Independent Designing: Where Do You Go from Here?

Using hypermedia for one project was fun and successful. Then we found that using hypermedia for more than one project saw all the benefits multiply and accrue. With this goal in mind, we changed our plans for our second quarter's unit on psychology. We decided to end the unit by having students design a hyperstack about a topic of their choice. This second hypermedia project, entitled "What Others Believe, Think, and Feel," would conclude our unit.

The purpose of this second project was to design a short hyperstack from scratch that would teach other students about an independently chosen topic from psychology. We would encourage students to anticipate their classmates' prior knowledge, interests, and the questions they would ask—and therefore the routes they might wish to take—as they read through the stack. We also decided to provide specific instructional support for organizing the stacks by asking students to create concept webs before creating their stacks.

Now that our students had a basic understanding of and facility with hypermedia tools, they could begin designing their own stacks. We hoped that they would begin exploring the connections among ideas and the possible "reads" or paths likely through those connections by their classmates.

This was not as much of a leap as it might seem. Their motivation was high. They had already learned the basic tools. And they had already been adding independently designed literary character cards to their personality stack by the time this second project was under way.

The Psychology Stack

For the remaining hypercard projects, we used the model of student design (cf. Chapter 3, Erickson 1997; Lehrer et al. 1994):

1. Chose a topic.
2. Ask questions about the topic.
3. Find and develop information.
4. Develop and revise the topic.
5. Analyze and examine information in detail.
6. Organize information.
7. Design a plan or outline.
8. Represent understandings to show what you know.
9. Reflect seriously on your information and design.
10. Refine to make the product more polished, accessible, and interesting to the audience.
11. Present your findings and products to others.

We began the psychology project by reviewing the use of hypermedia. The first student task was to build a short stack exploring a current event. (See Figure 4.5.) This took only a day or two.

During this psychology project and all that followed, all students created their own cards and links. Many students began to use the

FIGURE 4.5   O. J. Simpson practice stack template sheet.

Directions: Use the HyperCard tools to create a stack similar to the one below.

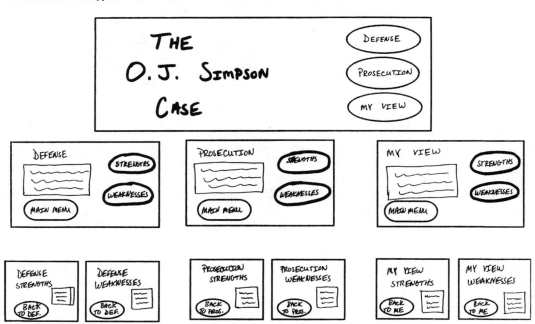

multimedia possibilities of hypermedia to represent information about their topic—experimenting with how audiovisual features and stack organization could contribute to the reader's experience and understanding of the text.

Jordan, who so much enjoyed the graphic elements of hypermedia, did only a mediocre job of writing about his topic, but his stack excited other students because he created an animated cartoon to represent the ideas of id and superego (see one of his flip cards in Figure 4.6).

In the cartoon, a boy is tortured by the conflicting advice given to him by his id, represented by a little devil, and his superego, represented by a little angel. The ego, housed in his brain, must balance these divisive desires and make a decision.

This inventive animation was typical of many disengaged learners: they became excited by the possibilities of the computer and found ways

FIGURE 4.6　Flip animation cards on ideas of id and superego. Subsequent cards show objects moved in relation to the previous cards so as to create the illusion of real movement.

to include some technological flash in their hypermedia compositions. We insisted, however, that the "flash" be justified and serve the overall communicative purposes of the stack. The students who began experimenting were often those considered at risk, and they became experts and advisers who helped other students with these design features.

We attached a designer's diary to each stack, which we began requiring as a part of every student hypercard document. Students used the diary daily to tell what they were doing as hypermedia designers, and why. We asked students to use the diary to reflect on and justify what they were doing and making (e.g., why they created the links that they did between cards). In this way, we tried to provide students with a place to reflect and record their thoughts, observations, questions, plans, activities, and justifications.

While creating his psychology stack, Jordan reflected on all of these issues in his design diary:

> 10/3—Superego is like angel. Id like devil. Ego has to decide. I will make animation cartoon. To show how decision is not easy and takes time.

> 10/4—Made drawings and pasted them on different cards, changing them to show things happening. Pictures could maybe be bigger but I like them.

> 10/5—Finished and showed cartoon. Joe thought it was cool. I asked him what it meant and he said that we want to be good and have fun and sometimes that's not the same thing so we have trouble deciding. So it worked OK.

We hoped to stimulate and encourage learner awareness of thinking skills, thereby promoting active learning and self-awareness, or metacognition (Flavell 1976). In this way, as well as through class work, students were expressly learning about their own learning.

Hypermedia documents can naturally include a learner diary, and it can be hidden behind the primary documents. The learner's diary becomes an explicit subtext of the project; students are asked to think about their thinking and reflect on their products as a natural part of the learning process. Throughout the projects, we asked students to make their reasoning visible and their decisions and knowledge accountable. They became better and better at this over time.

Cassie had no trouble generating information, diving immediately into her topic and creating a more sophisticated organization than she had used earlier by creating five subtopics of information about her topic of parapsychology. Two of her subtopics were further divided into subsub-

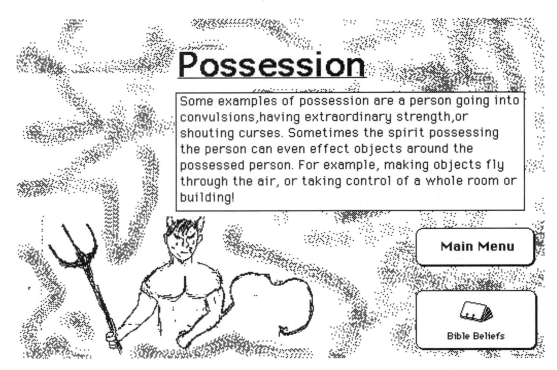

FIGURE 4.7　Printout of Possession card that shows cross-link to biblical beliefs and the the Biblical Beliefs card.

topics that explored examples or proponents of the cited phenomenon. The girl who had suffered from writer's block was suddenly in danger of endless hypercard permutation.

Mark surprised us by being the first student to create multiple semantic links. His stack explored the topic of occult uses of parapsychology. On his Possession card and several others, he referred readers to a separate stack about biblical explanations and admonitions regarding these phenomena. (See Figure 4.7.)

Cultural Journalism Project

Throughout the third quarter of the school year and on into April, students pursued a team-taught integrated research project in their language arts and social studies classes. The students divided into groups and chose a particular culture of interest to them: Native Americans; the cul-

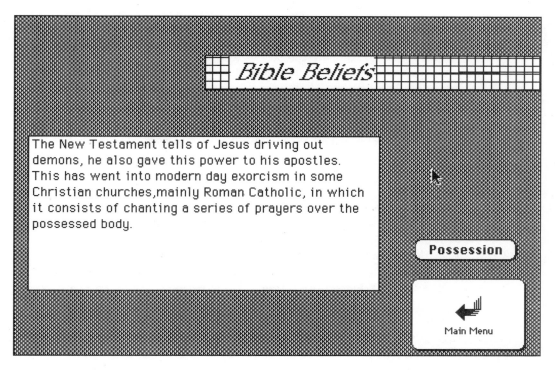

Figure 4.7 continued

ture of our own small town of Beaver Dam; the culture of a street gang; Hawaiian culture; the culture of Laos, a Native American tribe; Japan; a particular tribal culture in East Africa; Arabia; or mainstream culture in Scandinavia, Iceland, Germany, Italy, or another country. Each year, as we and our students revised the project, different kinds of questions and topics would be pursued.

We framed the project by asking students to create documents that could be put in the library and be useful to others. We brainstormed for possible audiences for their materials: other students, travel agents, tourists, exchange students, missionaries, trade missions, entrepreneurs, medical professionals, history buffs, and others. What kinds of things would these people need to know? Which of these issues were most interesting to the students? We then asked them to design a document about their culture that was compelling to them and would address the needs and concerns of one of these groups.

Each group asked questions about their culture topic that they wanted to answer and present to their classmates and the future audiences they had selected. They began to find information in the library, on CDs, on video, and through artwork. Each group invited at least one informant from the culture or who had lived in that culture. These visitors came to our school and were interviewed. Eventually the groups divided their topics into subtopics and began to create subtopic stacks. By reading each other's stacks, they began to make links between the stacks. We allotted six weeks for the project and eventually used nearly eleven weeks for it. Significant learning and learning projects take time. We must reconceive of how we use time in school if we are to improve education.

This first year, when the cultural journalism unit had been completed and the dust was beginning to settle, Paul said to me: "What more is there to do? What we just did could be the whole curriculum for school, K through 12."

I asked him to explain.

"The kids learned how to find information, organize it, represent it, and refine it. What more do they need to know about learning and communicating that couldn't be taught through this thing?"

Paul had a point that would be echoed by many curriculum theorists and researchers on integrated education (Beane 1990; Brazee 1995; Lounsbury 1996; Wood et al. 1997). Yet it's important to remember that such projects can be implemented in more traditional notions of curriculum to consolidate more circumscribed concepts and skills. Although our curriculum came to the point where it was driven by the notion of design, this model can be used in much shorter and ancillary ways, with great benefits to teachers and students.

During this project, Cassie and Mark were members of a four-student team creating a stack on Italy. After they generated a list of questions they wanted answered about Italian culture, Cassie decided to address several issues under the topic of Family Life, with an eye toward informing future exchange students. While researching this topic, she learned to make spaghetti and lasagna noodles from scratch and made recipe cards. She learned the slang names for twelve different kinds of noodles (e.g., rotini = sewer pipes). She learned that the father sits at the head of the table and gets to eat out of the big pasta bowl after everyone else has served themselves. Why? Because the bowl will have the most sauce, which the father deserves. She discovered that there are several different Italian cuisines, all with their particular types of wines and pastas, and she provided menus one might find in different parts of Italy. And this was just the subtopic of Eating Habits. Cassie was having no more trouble thinking about what to write or where to go next.

Meanwhile, Mark was in the sort of trouble so typical for him, but this time he had a way of getting out of it. His first tree, a tool to organize his topic, was a mess. He was describing the free market economy of Italy. As just one example of his problem, he included "money system" and "the lira" as subtopics on a stack called Major Industries.

During our initial conference with Mark, we asked him what an Italian exchange student in the seventh grade might ask him about our economy. "Is he going to care about what we call the economy or about inflationary pressures?" Paul asked him. "I only know about that stuff because I studied it in college."

Mark went around to several students from other groups and asked what they would want to know about the Italian economy. His list had these questions:

- What kind of interesting jobs do people have in Italy?
- What do they do with their money?
- What happens if you don't have a job?
- How are prices for things different than here in the United States?
- What affects earning and spending power in Italy?

Mark's resulting stack on jobs had cards about the fashion industry, making race cars, wine tasting, and the influence of the mafia. (See Figure 4.8.) "This was a lot more fun to do than what I was going to do," he admitted. "And a lot more fun to read," I added. In addition, it served the purpose for his targeted audience of an exchange student.

When all five stacks from his group were put together, Mark began to make links from his stack to those of other group members. His Earning Power card was connected in two different ways to Eddie's Education stack, which featured advanced education and job opportunities. His Inflation card about the changing value of the lira was connected to a card from the stack on Government, and his Mafia card to the Government substack on fighting crime.

"Wow, I can't believe how much all of our stacks have to do with each other," he told me. He was finally making connections among topic content while also developing research and literacy skills.

Jordan's stack on the leisure pursuits of East Africa was passable in that he had five cards describing the rules of various games. It was a success in that he had completed his stack on his own with little help. But it seemed

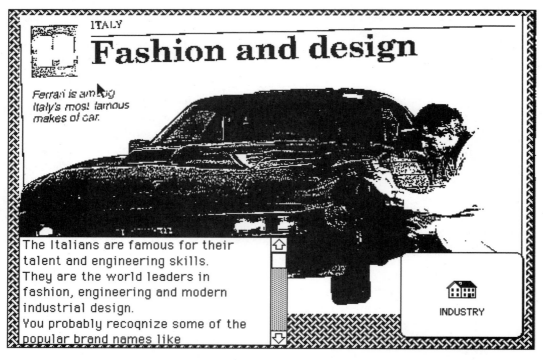

FIGURE 4.8   Cards about the fashion industry and cars from Italy.

uninspired and showed only a few simple links. There were no subtopics or links made to other stacks. Especially disappointing was that he failed to include several leisure pursuits explicitly shared with him by two East African visitors to our school. The course of learning does not run smoothly or quickly. These cognitive skills are difficult to learn, require much assistance over time, and take much time to develop—which is precisely why we continued to teach and support the skills in the context of ever more challenging projects (Erickson and Lehrer, in press).

The Final Exam

At the end of the year, when we thought that what would be achieved had been achieved, Jordan made a quantum leap in his hypermedia design.

For the final exam in social studies, we asked students to choose any topic studied during the year and create a stack about how that topic plays itself out in their individual lives. Students chose their topics three

Fashion Cars

The Italians make some of the most exciting and creative cars in the world.The most well known cars are the Lamborghini and the Ferrari. The most bought fashion car in Italy though is the Alpha romero.

To Fashion

Figure 4.8 continued

days before the exam. The intervening three days were for gathering and organizing information. The final exam period of seventy minutes was for creating the stack.

Cassie did a stack on study skills and included various tips and formats to help her audience. Mark did a great job on the genealogy of his family, and his hyperstack organization reflected that of a family tree.

Jordan created his best work of the year. He created a stack about the local culture. For the first time, he divided subtopics into connected substacks on historical sites into Indian sites and Modern sites, and cultural institutions into government and the arts. The Government stack included cards on the governing of localities and the state. His stack on sports and recreation included explanations about reel and fly fishing, ice hockey, and cross-country skiing (but despite his sister, no discussion of figure skating!).

All of our 125 students completed their stacks to the satisfaction of our criteria; seventeen students stayed after the exam hour or came after school (on the last day) to finish and present their stacks to our faculty panel. This in itself was amazing to us.

When students engage in questions of personal relevance and make knowledge artifacts to share with others, they not only are motivated to complete their work, but are motivated and can be helped to do ever more sophisticated work. That is what learning should be all about.

Chapter 5

Beginning the Inquiry Process

Important Points

This chapter describes how student motivation was sustained through an extended cultural journalism unit and how important skills of questioning and finding information were taught in the context of this unit. It concludes by explaining how to keep track of student work during extended projects as you keep students on track.

➥ Curriculum is everything that students do in school.

➥ In the cultural journalism unit featured here:

  ▪ School curriculum was used as the starting point for unit planning.

  ▪ Student needs, prior knowledge, and interests were taken into account.

  ▪ Front-loading activities were used to motivate students to participate fully in all unit activities, activate students' prior knowledge and experiences that would help them to connect to the unit, and build background information that they would need to understand fully the readings and activities.

  ▪ Important concepts were pursued together so that students would have a common set of understandings for pursuing their different group inquiries.

  ▪ Student questions about the unit theme were elicited and foregrounded.

➥ Motivation was sustained by (1) addressing issues of personal relevance and social significance, (2) emphasizing why the unit goals were important, (3) devising a project that resulted in a useful product, (4) naming student competence, (5) providing continual feedback, (6) allowing for choice, and (7) making the work both challenging and fun.

➥ Students were helped to understand what good groups do to ensure productive working relationships.

➥ Students were assisted to ask important researchable questions through K-W-L, roundtable critiques, the creation of help sheets and learning guides, and the provision of multiple levels of assistance.

➥ Students were guided to find various kinds of text, electronic, and nontextual forms of information.

➥ Various procedures like entrance and exit slips, project checksheets, journals, and design diaries helped everyone monitor and keep track of progress and to know what they had done and what they needed to do. Everyone shared a responsibility for keeping track of learning.

➥ The skills learned here are those needed in any kind of inquiry, whether that inquiry results in a hypermedia document, a video document, a written paper, or some other form of representing what has been learned. All of the skills emphasized in this chapter are useful in all other learning situations involving inquiry.

What any person in the world can learn, almost all persons can learn *if* provided with appropriate and prior conditions of learning.

Benjamin Bloom (1976, p. 7)

The Question is everything, because inquiring minds want to know!

Sean, seventh grader, from his design diary

A man's reach should exceed his grasp, or what's a heaven for?

Robert Browning

This and the next four chapters demonstrate how we taught and "apprenticed" our students as researchers and learners through the course of our cultural journalism project, our most extended project each year. Although we use this particular unit to show how we taught particular skills and strategies in practice, the skill sequences could easily be adapted for use with other kinds of units and other kinds of projects, even ones that result in more traditional products, such as a written report or term paper.

Creating Curriculum

Most classrooms are driven by content curriculum. Students are taught information in each subject area as determined by the school's curriculum guide. But the deeper we became involved in student-design learning projects, the more we came to conceive of the curriculum not as content but as experiences to support the gaining of cognitive skills and procedures that lead to autonomous thinking. These procedures helped our students to develop ways of learning and dealing with the concepts of the school curriculum.

When we began our integrated cultural journalism project several years ago, we conscientiously followed the content-area curricula. For example, we required that each student group create stacks on the five cultural institutions: political/judicial, economic/occupational, educational, religious, and familial institutions. Through the years, our ideas and practices have evolved. Now, groups might introduce an overview of cultural institutions, but their stacks focus much more deeply on issues of personal concern—ideas like taboos, sport, and leisure activities. For example, one girl covered economy/industry under her chosen topic of the importance of fashion. She demonstrated her understanding of a cultural institution and how this institution related to other institutions. In this way, the school's curricular goals were met, and so were our goals for student learning and her goals for personal relevance.

We've always begun the cultural journalism unit with overview activities such as personal reflections, with drama activities involving different cultural perspectives, with value surveys, and the like. We start with the students themselves, and how they, their families, and peer groups express culture. This preparatory work served to activate students' relevant background knowledge and helped to activate and develop knowledge necessary to dealing with the materials of the unit. It also helped students to connect personally to the topic. We call this kind of work *front-loading.*

We then pursued readings and other activities to provide students with a firm grounding of central cultural concepts. (For a more extended discussion of this preparatory work, see Wilhelm and Edmiston 1998.) These activities were designed to help students to define the notion and importance of culture. We wanted them to understand that a culture includes a value system; habits of thought; assumptions about reality and knowledge; language; preferences in art, foods, fashion, and expression; leisure pursuits; and ways of organizing and giving meaning to human activity. We also wanted them to understand that the existence of different cultures and subcultures can lead to interpersonal and intergroup conflict and to intrapersonal conflict, which need to be addressed.

After a week and a half of such activities in social studies and language arts classes, students shared enough general background knowledge to select cultural topics and begin articulating research questions to inform their own research.

Jump-starting the Kids: Motivating Factors

All of our inquiry projects through the year, but particularly this one on cultural journalism, required a huge commitment from the students in terms of sustained time, interest, and energy. We therefore put several key principles into play to motivate their work throughout the units:

1. Students helped to set the purposes of the project.
2. The purpose included the creation of products and artifacts that would be used to communicate with and teach others, and to enact some kind of social action.
3. Student competence and improvement were identified and emphasized.
4. Continuous feedback was provided from multiple sources.
5. The work was social and fun.
6. Choice was foregrounded.

Purpose Setting

We attempted to justify our units of study to the students in terms that connected them to the importance of the material. We framed this unit as being about the importance of culture as a way of organizing and lending meaning to our communal lives, and of understanding cultural perspectives as a way of solving conflicts and enriching ourselves. When the students began their own inquiries, they were allowed to choose their own groups and ask research questions of personal interest and relevance about a cultural topic. They also identified the audience and purpose of their final product. We believe that students need to know why they should know and do things. We also believe that they need to use what they are learning in a context that is significant to them (Bruer 1993).

Creation of Real Products

This kind of knowledge development is most powerful when kids use what they have learned to make real artifacts that serve real purposes (diSessa 1992; Harel and Papert 1991; Lehrer et al. 1994). The products were viewed by multiple audiences, and often worked to achieve or inspire some kind of change of opinion or socially oriented action.

Competence

We arranged our work so that students would continually reflect on, return to, and refine central processes of learning. Eventually, they would use both hypermedia tools and learning strategies independently, as when they created video documentaries during our final Civil Rights and Social Justice Unit (see Chapter 9). The modeling, coaching, and then the fading of assistance helped students become autonomous. By our naming what students could do, setting goals, and helping them to monitor and articulate how they were improving, students achieved a sense of growing competence that was highly motivating. The hypermedia platform made what they had learned visible and tangible to them, so that their learning was clearly displayed to themselves and others.

Feedback

As students used what they were learning in meaningful contexts, they received continuous feedback from teachers, peers, and the document they were creating. They saw the results of their learning. The documents were intended for real audiences, and the students would eventually present their work to these audiences, which encouraged purposefulness, authenticity, and feedback (Carver et al. 1992).

Fun

Bloom's research (1985) on the development of talent demonstrates that having fun when particular kinds of ideas or inquiry are introduced significantly affects the kind of interest and engagement students later display. Therefore, we often used drama and gamelike structures to introduce and frame our work, and to teach mini-lessons during the course of a project. We wanted the work to have an element of play and encouraged experimentation and group work. We believe that there is a kind of "hard fun" (Papert 1996) that results from answering significant questions, creating and representing knowledge, meeting intellectual and emotional challenges, and helping each other to grasp what may lie just beyond our reach.

Importance of Choice

Each year we have provided students with more choice in the content that they will pursue. Our classroom research indicates that this increased latitude of choice has resulted in our students' learning more content, achieving higher standards of design, and being more motivated to go above and beyond the standards that they have articulated for the project. Giving up a measure of teacher control seems to have encouraged students to pursue issues of greater and greater interest, which has motivated them and made for better learning and thinking.

We have talked about this phenomenon on several occasions and about how passionately many of our students, particularly those who might be considered at risk, have pursued these design projects. On reflection, it does seem natural that a core element of any love or passion involves choice—an exercise of independence in meeting one's own needs. Changing the rules provides motivation for at-risk kids and gives them many ways to participate legitimately in what they see as important tasks.

Various studies of American education (Goodlad 1984) have demonstrated that American students are generally disaffected and disengaged, so much that Csikszentmihalyi and Larson (1984) have argued that most students, most of the time, feel alienated from schooling, even in schools considered to be exemplary. These researchers state that "schools are essentially machines for providing negative feedback. They are supposed to reduce deviances, to constrain the behavior and the minds of adolescents within straight and narrow channels" (pp. 198–199).

Several important studies have demonstrated that students become highly motivated and engaged when they are encouraged to plan, do, and create projects of personal relevance that value, privilege, and extend what they already know (Csikszentmihalyi, Rathunde, and Whalen 1993; Heath and McLaughlin 1993). Csikszentmihalyi and his coauthors describe this high absorption in learning as a "flow" experience. They found that when students describe what allows for such absorption, they do not mention extrinsic kinds of motivation like recognition or money, but instead focus on intrinsic rewards like enjoyment, personal interest and relevance, challenge, and satisfaction in meeting challenges.

Benjamin Bloom's work (1976) on potential indicates that students of all abilities are much more likely to actualize their potential in authentic learning scenarios than they are in traditional school settings. Hillocks (1995) argues that this "means that we need to forget about generalized notions of intelligence and aptitude and concern ourselves instead with working out where students are in relation to specific learning tasks, what students have to know to accomplish that, and how they can enjoy learning those things" (p. 22). This was the challenge we undertook.

Choosing Groups

Our students worked on these projects in groups of three to five. Grouping students was always a problem, but predicated on our dedication to student choice, we allowed students as much responsibility as possible for making such decisions—as much as possible, that is, without relinquishing our responsibility to make sure things worked.

By the time the cultural journalism project rolled around at the beginning of the second semester, students had worked in a variety of groups that they had been assigned to and that they had chosen. These groups included peer editing groups, shared reading groups, reading pairs, and groups who had worked together on a variety of short drama projects, news shows, and other kinds of projects. We had also taken time in our classes to reflect on what kinds of attitudes and behaviors helped groups to work, and what kinds of behaviors and issues hindered a group's work. We spent time developing positive group behaviors and reflecting on our own group work.

We first asked individual students to identify possible cultural topics to pursue, and then asked them to form groups of individuals whom they thought would work well together and shared similar research interests. For all of the longer group projects, including this one, we allowed students the freedom to apply to become a group. Part of this application required them to articulate standards for a good group and to list what group member qualities would be necessary to complete this extended project successfully. If we had any concerns about a group, that group had to respond to them in writing and make a clear case that their group would be successful. If they could not convince us, their group needed to reconfigure. With a minimum of inevitable last-minute shuffling and an occasional group that petitioned to work in a pair, this way of forming groups seemed to work quite well.

Group Issues

Although adolescents generally enjoy working with their peers, there were occasional students or parents who voiced concerns about working in a group for an entire grading period. They were often concerned that one integrated project would account for the third-quarter grade in two classes. We addressed these concerns by balancing individual and group assessment, as well as process and product evaluations. (See Chapters 7 and 8 for more on this subject.) We also argued forcefully for the importance of working in groups.

On rare occasions, an individual student would not be part of any group applications. We worked to avoid this by making it clear that we had a responsibility to work with others and welcome classmates who shared our research interests into our groups. We also provided class time for students to talk about forming groups. When a student did have trouble finding a suitable group, we asked the person what group he or she would most like to join, and then we met with that group privately to ask that they invite the individual to work with them.

It also happened that after a first round of research, a group member would decide that the topic or the situation was no longer appealing. Usually the person had an idea of a group in mind with whom to work. We would ask this person to speak with both groups, and if agreement could be reached, we would approve the move. Throughout, we asked students to be responsible for themselves, to address all problems with all involved, and to be fair and flexible with each other. This was often difficult, but these are important lessons for all of us to learn.

Group Benefits

The benefits of working together are great. Vogt (1985) and Tharp and Gallimore (1990) have called the activity setting of project collaboration the most powerful source of learning assistance, for both children and adults. Tharp and Gallimore (1990), using Vygotsky, demonstrate that self-regulating thought comes from the "intersubjectivity" (entering and taking on the thought patterns of others) achieved through group sharing and from the stress and disruption caused to individual ways of thinking through the exchange and challenge encountered in groups. For these reasons, and our firm belief that learning is a dialogic and action-oriented activity (Bakhtin 1986), we proceeded with the use of learning groups for this extended project.

Although group solidarity and collegiality were generally high, we found that asking the students to choose and justify their groupings and to create a group name or mascot did a lot to help the groups gel. Once groups and general cultural topics were chosen, we were ready to proceed to asking particular questions about the chosen topic.

Priming the Pump: Asking Personally Relevant Questions

All learning must be achieved from the starting point of a student's current knowledge and interest (Beane 1990). When Jordan chose to pursue the question of how games and sports expressed the tribal cultures of East Africa, he was building on his own interests and experience as a hockey player and attempting to connect personally to his studies. Cassie, in asking about the importance of cooking and cuisine to the social and family life of Italy, was also building on and attempting to extend her personal interests. In both cases, we were able to use the topics these students had selected to build cultural knowledge and teach them how to use tools for asking questions, finding and analyzing information, and so forth. These processes helped them to answer their own questions, proceed with pleasure, and be prepared for similar pursuits in the future.

Educational research suggests that students often have difficulty relating new knowledge to old knowledge (Bruer 1993). For example, difficulties in reading comprehension have been shown to be caused much more often by the failure to access prior knowledge (or schema—an organized set of knowledge around an idea) than a failure to decode and comprehend words (Bruer 1993; Byrnes 1996).

Therefore, front-loading activities that help students to articulate what they already know and still need to know are essential to help them activate schemas and relate what they already know to new material. In addition, this gives teachers a basis for instruction. By finding out what students were thinking, we could more easily gauge where students needed to go and how to assist them. This was repeatedly made obvious to us during these projects. For example, we helped our East Africa group to brainstorm what they knew about Native American tribes and tribal culture to help them understand the nature of Kenyan politics. Once they began to learn about tribal groups, political power, employment, personal income, population density, crime, and pollution, they immediately began to ask questions about the relationships among these ideas: How does the political power of particular tribes like the Masai and Kikuyu translate into employment and income? How is population density related to employment? to crime and pollution? The students would never have thought to ask and explore these questions until they had begun to learn about these issues and connect them to their previous experience and knowledge. It would also be impossible for them to conduct directed information searches about tribal groups and political leaders until they knew the names for them, which they learned from their initial research forays. As teachers, we had a lot of work to do to help students articulate their prior knowledge and get started.

Without prior knowledge, interest, and engagement, no amount of support would enable reluctant students in our classrooms to do the hard work that would move them beyond their current independent levels of achievement.

Asking Researchable Questions

To help students articulate and refine researchable questions that were engaging, personally relevant, and significant, we supported them through the following activities.

Step 1: Generating Questions with K-W-L

To help groups ask questions about their topic, students used the K-W-L model (Ogle 1983). Group members listed what they knew (K) and wanted to learn (W) about their culture and began to brainstorm questions of interest. (L) is a citation of what they had learned once the research questions were pursued.

Step 2: Organizing Questions with Question Webs

Using these brainstormed questions, we worked with the students to create question webs of potential research questions.

We started the process of producing question webs by discussing and defining seed questions. Students were encouraged to remember them as the 5 W's and an H: who, what, when, why, where, and how? Students were asked to brainstorm all the possible questions they had about their topic. Then they began to categorize questions into groups or patterns based on what they had previously learned about culture in general. The research question or general topic was placed in the middle of a sheet of paper and the categories branched off it, like a web. Under each category, the list of questions was placed. Figure 5.1 shows a web.

Step 3: Defining Purposes and an Audience for the Research

At this time, we began to work with the groups to frame the purposes and audiences of their research. Certainly a primary aim was to satisfy their own curiosity about particular issues and make personal connections to a culture different from their own. But we also wanted the document they created to be socially significant, in that it would serve a real-world pur-

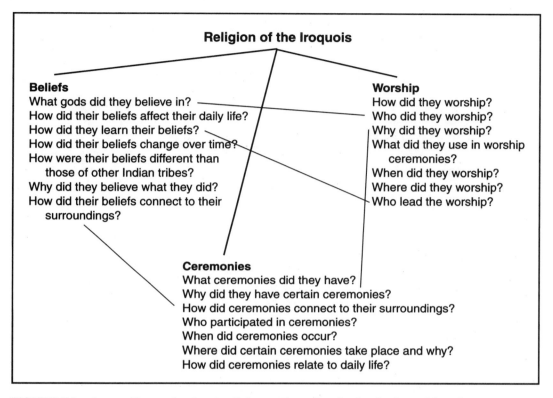

FIGURE 5.1 A question web of potential questions for the beginning of inquiry.

pose and teach readers something fundamental that they didn't already know. Beyond the personally meaningful rooting and context of the project, something real and useful was going to be created for real audiences, both inside and outside of the school.

We have found this creation of a real product to be important to the group work. This is supported by various strands of research (Carver et al. 1992; Lehrer 1993; Tharp and Gallimore 1990). Tharp and Gallimore write,

> For these younger children, though, a real product of a mural, a bulletin board, a painting, or a play will energize the activity immeasurably. And for content-area instruction and more mature students, it becomes necessary to arrange some use of the acquired knowledge, some application of the concepts, some product to either follow the learning conversations or accompany it. All carvers must have a canoe—idle talk palls. (p. 135)

This is one way in which school often differs from real-world learning. In the world, we strive to answer questions that concern us, and we learn so that we can know and *do* things with what we know.

We began to explore how answering our research questions might lead to the creation of products useful to real audiences. For example, the Italy group decided to create a travel guide for tourists, businesspeople, and exchange students traveling to Italy for longer stays. Their general question became: What would a person need to know to "thrive instead of survive" during a long stay in Italy? (Students like rhymes and sloganlike messages.) This led to subquestions like Cassie's about the importance of cooking and cuisine to Italian family and social life, and Mark's variety of questions about interesting jobs, unemployment, and prices in Italy.

The students were therefore creating real documents for real audiences beyond those of their classmates and reading buddies. We call this kind of work *framing* or putting a *drama frame* onto the work at hand. It provides a sense of audience, lends an air of seriousness to the efforts, aids purpose, and seems to make the learning more fun. It is akin to Heathcote's (Heathcote and Bolton 1995) notion of the "mantle of the expert" drama technique, which casts students as experts with a task to perform. A drama frame is a powerful tool for creating mental models and helping students to use information to solve real-world problems that may be distant from them in time and space. (For full discussions of both framing and the use of drama to assist learning across the curriculum, see Wilhelm and Edmiston 1998.) This framing provides purpose and perspective to the work at hand and helps things to get started and maintain focus.

Step 4: Refining Researchable Questions

Now questioning began to take on a serious edge. We provided students with a questioning guide (see Figure 5.2) to help them formalize the questions they had been brainstorming. The guide we used was adapted from Julie Erickson and Anne Haase, and we tweaked it each year based on the students' input about effective questions. It was important that the group had a general research question that would be answered by each of the group member's more specific questions. Also important was that these questions were compelling and researchable.

Once students had generated revised webs of possible questions for their substack, they would present these questions in roundtables made up of members from other groups. (This idea came from Rich Lehrer and

Asking Questions: A Guide for Students

Criteria for Asking Questions

You can ask if

- You begin by asking numerous questions—*brainstorm!* (During brainstorming, you don't evaluate your questions—just generate them.)
- You can use *seed questions* (who, what, when, where, why, how), especially if you get stuck during brainstorming.
- After brainstorming, you *categorize* your questions.
- Your categorized questions have *headings* that describe what they have in common.
- You *evaluate* your questions to see if they should be refined (to make the wording clearer, few yes/no answers, combine questions, etc.).
- Your questions are neither too broad nor too narrow.
- You evaluate your questions and *select* a limited number of research questions.

Tips

1. Pick a topic you are interested in. You will be researching it for a long time.
2. Consider the possible answers to your questions. Are they one word (too narrow)? Can you find information about it (are the questions answerable)?
3. When asking questions, keep in mind the *task*; how are you supposed to present or share the information?
4. After brainstorming, organize your questions and *clarify* them. Your questions are the basis of your research.
5. Keep in mind what kind of information you may find.

If Stuck...

- Use seed questions.
- Change the topic to one you're really interested in.
- Ask a history question (where did something come from, what did it look like when it first started, how has it changed...).

Tips for Categorizing Your Questions

- Think about what is similar about some of the questions.
- Put the questions that are similar into separate groups.
- Try to come up with a *keyword* or name that describes each category.
- Sometimes the categories are subtopics to your topic of interest. If so, this subtopic name could be the name of a category.

FIGURE 5.2   Questioning guide handout given to students.

Julie.) In a roundtable, students would present their current work and have it critiqued. Again, we provided structures and feedback for positive group interaction. Using a technique called P-Q-P, each critic first had to provide *praise* for the question list (or whatever else had been produced), then ask *questions* about it, and finally offer suggestions for *polishing* or improving what had been created. (We became familiar with the P-Q-P technique through our work with the National Writing Project.)

Each critic had the responsibility of providing all three kinds of feedback. We would start off with one volunteer's putting his list on the overhead. In a large group, we would all write and share our critiques to provide a model of the kind of activity that should ensue in the smaller groups. Group work would proceed for a class period. At this point, we would gather data from each roundtable group about the conclusions they had reached about researchable questions and good question lists. This would consist of the group's written standards for such questions and a revised list of questions. Then a class guide would be created to supplement the previously disseminated teacher-generated guide (see Figure 5.3).

FIGURE 5.3   Class-created guide on researchable questions and good question lists to replace the teacher-generated guide.

Questioning Objectives

1. Can *brainstorm* to activate prior knowledge (K-W-L).
2. Can ask *seed questions* (who, what, where, when, why, how).
3. Can ask *different sorts* of questions (QAR).
4. Can *differentiate* between good, poor, appropriate, and inappropriate questions.

Good Questions
- Are challenging.
- Point out key details needed to know to understand content.
- Are specific enough so person clearly understands what is being asked.
- Make you use your imagination.
- Put you in another person's place or give you the perspective of another person.
- Cause you to relate the situation to your own life or experiences and make you think how you personally could or would be affected.

Food for Thought
How do you change poor questions into good ones?
Think about something you can read that is related to your culture.

Step 5: Finalizing the Questions

Through a sequence of such activities, the students were guided to a point after two days where they had negotiated a general group question and a variety of substack questions that would help to answer the general question. For example, the Italy group had asked the general question: What do people need to know to thrive instead of just survive during a long-term visit to Italy? Subquestions revolved around what needed to be known about cuisine, the world of work, the culture surrounding sports, dating, and others. Here is a partial list of questions that members of the Italy group took to their respective roundtables:

1. What is the economics of Italy?
2. What do people eat in Italy?
3. What if you were a foreign exchange student in Italy?
4. What are the major industries in Italy?
5. What are the major entertainments in Italy?
6. What does "Italy" mean?
7. What should I do and see on a visit to Italy?
8. Describe the history of Italy.

In one roundtable the group immediately critiqued the third question: What if you were a foreign exchange student to Italy? They identified this as the group's general question. "Why don't you just say: 'What do you need to know to successfully fit in as a foreign exchange student to Italy, or a businessman or whatever?'" one girl advised Cassie. On the other hand, the group critiqued the question: What do people eat in Italy? as too narrow. One boy had this to say: "Yeah, that tells you what you might want to eat or be prepared to eat when you go, but what about their habits, or where they eat, or when, and stuff like that? I mean there are all kinds of interesting and important stuff around eating that this question really misses."

The question: What is the economics of Italy? was critiqued as too general to be helpful, and the group brainstormed more specific and audience-friendly questions. This group decided that a question had to fit and help answer the group's general question. Questions could be too narrow or too general to achieve this end, be "right on!" or "totally off the mark!" Their classification scheme of question critiques, developed during the roundtables with the help of teacher coaching, was similar to what many other groups came up with.

As a result of the roundtable process of figuring out what to critique and then applying these standards, Cassie was helped to generate specific questions to help her with her substack on cuisine, and she took suggestions back to Mark for his substack on the economy of Italy. Mark was not as receptive to the advice he received from Cassie's roundtable or from his own roundtable as were the other members of his design group. Still, good suggestions had been made, and we were able to follow up on them. Sometimes experiencing things over and over from different perspectives is what fosters deep learning (Byrnes 1996).

Step 6: Revising and Refining the Research Questions

Even once students settled on very useful research questions, we stressed that questions often change and evolve through the research process. In fact, we often revisited and revised questions through conferencing, reflective journals, and other means. The question became the driving force behind all the work that followed, and we continued to pay a lot of attention to students' research questions, because they provided the purpose and focus of all subsequent work.

Finding Information: Addressing the Questions

The next step in the process was to find information that addressed the research question.

Step 1: Bookpasses

We began with strategies for finding information through nonelectronic sources by engaging in bookpasses (Erickson and Lehrer, in press). In a *bookpass,* we passed around books that possessed cultural information. Each student would have the chance to study a book, periodical, or other text for about ninety seconds before having to pass it on and receive a new book. Students were to record what kind of information could be gleaned from the texts they had viewed. In this way, students discussed and traded ideas with us and each other about sources of print information, titles, indexes, tables of contents, headers, and other conventions for organizing texts and helping readers to find textual information. We followed up with mini-lessons on indexes and other kinds of textual features whenever we felt it was necessary.

Step 2: Brainstorming and Using Keywords and Related Terms

At this point we passed out our learning guide for finding information (all of our guides are based on the work of Ann Haase and Julie) and began to brainstorm keywords and related terms that would help students find information related to their topic. We now began to do electronic searches, with multimedia encyclopedias and non-Internet sources such as TOM. More recently, we have helped students to use the same techniques to find information online.

The notion of web-based information searches highlights many issues that are of concern, though perhaps less urgently, with any kind of information search:

1. Does the school have an AUP (acceptable use policy) for cruising the Internet; have the student and a parent signed it; and is the student adhering to the agreement? (For a full discussion of the importance of AUPs and how to implement them, see Power, Wilhelm, and Chandler 1997.)
2. Given the research question, is this an appropriate site to visit?
3. Who are the authors of this page, and do they have credibility? What is the authors' agenda and perspective, and does it fit our own? How have they made their information accountable?
4. Can the information here be verified or "triangulated" with other sources, such as print and expert informant sources?

In an age when anyone can post anything on her own home page, students need to be helped to apply critical standards for what counts as knowledge. They need to consider rigorously what can be accepted and what needs to be verified. Of course, this is true of all information, whatever the source, but the issue is particularly important when dealing with web-based sources.

Step 3: Finding Diverse Sources of Information

We always require students to collect information from nontextual sources. It was important to us that they did not regard the web or the library as the only places to find interesting information. Each group had to collect and study artifacts such as artwork, menus, foodstuffs, magazines, clothing, videotapes, musical albums, and other exhibits that would help them to gain some contextual understanding of their culture and their research questions regarding it. We also required them to read stories and myths and to become familiar with folklore important in the culture. We collected quite a few anthologies of such stories, and made use of the International Co-operative Children's Book Center (4920 Helen C. White Hall, University of Wisconsin-Madison, Madison, WI 53706) as a resource. This required some advanced planning; many wonderful resources could be ordered through interlibrary loans, but they took some time to arrive.

Groups were also asked to write letters to embassies and other cultural organizations that could provide information. It was always exciting to students when they received packets from an Inuit cultural society in Greenland or the Kenyan embassy. This was also an opportunity to learn and use formal letter writing skills, again applying skills for authentic purposes, to get information instead of just to practice letter writing.

Step 4: Finding an Informant

One of the most exciting aspects of the projects for our students was the requirement that they contact and meet with a cultural informant for an interview. The local state university was a great help in setting us up with informants from a variety of cultures. Sometimes we had to settle for nonnative informants—people who had been tourists or who had served in the Peace Corps in various venues. Human informants are always a valuable resource, no matter the inquiry topic. They bring the community into the classroom and model for students the variety of interests and expertise that exist within the community.

The students first had to find and then contact the informant through a phone call to arrange an interview, and to confirm and provide directions. Usually there were some informants who could not drive to our rural school, so each year we made one or two after-school trips with various groups to the state capital, where the students were able to meet and interview their informants.

As with all phases of the design process, students needed help developing new skills before practicing these skills. Motivation to learn about interviewing was high because skills were learned in a context of need. The students knew they would soon be interviewing an informant, knew who the informant was, and knew that the information they gathered was crucial to the creation of their document.

Before the actual interview, we role-played various interviewing scenarios in class. We role-played interviewees who answered in monosyllables and discussed ways to tease information out of people and get them to talk. We postured as informants who went off on tangents and discussed strategies for keeping people on track. We predicted other possible problems and dramatized them. At the end of this session, we created an interviewing guide and generated interview questions (see Figure 5.4).

The contacts made during interviews were tremendously exciting for students, proved to be a major source of information, and led to ever more collaborative relationships between school and community.

One year, we had a group studying Icelandic culture. Although they had been warned it might be difficult to find information on Iceland, they persevered, mostly because one boy's father had been stationed in Iceland during his air force duty. Contacting a university department on foreign languages led them to an Icelandic woman studying at the university. I took the group to her home one afternoon, and they were served an Icelandic-style coffee with a cheese torte, saw a slide show, were provided with sacks full of books, and were then served an Icelandic dinner. After dinner they conducted their interview. They returned to school with a tremendous amount of information and a newfound enthusiasm.

This feature of the project encouraged us to break down the barriers between school and community. Many members of our own and surrounding communities willingly gave their time and energy to help our students. Some put together programs and slide shows that were so impressive we asked them to present to the whole seventh grade. A nice development was that as people became more aware of this annual project, they would call us to volunteer their own names or those of other resources whom they thought could help us.

More recently, students have been encouraged to find electronic informants. There are various search mechanisms and support services on the web to help students match up with experts in their area of inquiry. It is astonishing how small the world has become through the Internet and how available wonderful informants are to students.

One of the many web sites we recently used is Electronic Experts-Emissary-Electronic Mentors at the University of Texas-Austin, which can be found at http://www.tapr.org/emissary/. This site matches students to experts who are willing to help with student questions and research. The International E-mail Classroom Connection hosted at St. Olaf College entertains requests for informants from other cultures. The address is http://www.stolaf.edu/network/iecc/. This site also has an archive of lessons and projects that students might make use of that involve an exploration of cultural diversity. By using reputable sites that you have

Student Guide to Interviews

Most people think that interviews are easy because you just sit down and talk to someone. Well, there's a lot more to interviewing than that. Here are some tips to help you make your interviews worthwhile and fun.

Before the Interview

1. Brainstorm a list of potential questions and then decide which ones are most important to ask. Remember, people may have only a little time to spend with you.
2. Phrase your questions so that the response cannot be only "yes" or "no."
3. Ask "good" questions—interesting questions that you really want to know about.
4. Decide upon the time and place for the interview. If you need a pass from a teacher, make arrangements before the day of the interview.
5. Let the person know ahead of time the purpose for the interview and the topics that you hope to discuss.
6. Plan ahead to check out a tape recorder or video camera if you plan to use one. Practice with it before the interview. If you decide not to tape the interview, be sure to bring paper and pencil with you to the interview to take notes.
7. Practice asking questions on a family member, adult, or friend.

During the Interview

1. If you are using a video- or audiotape, be sure to ask the person if it is OK if you tape the interview. You must get permission. If you are not taping the interview, be sure to take notes.
2. Begin with questions that people will find interesting to answer.
3. Ask specific questions so that people don't get off track.
4. Keep eye contact. Notice body language and facial expressions.
5. Reflect answers to be sure that you have understood what the person is trying to say—for example, "So you are saying that…" or "So you mean that…"

6. Show that you are actively involved and listening by nodding or adding an occasional "yes" or "oh" or "that's very interesting."
7. Don't interrupt unless it is very important.
8. Follow up interesting responses with more questions—for example, "Could you give me an example of that?" or "How does that relate to what you said before?"
9. After you're done, thank the person by saying, "Thank you for your time" or "Thanks for spending time with me today" or "I appreciate your doing the interview."

After the Interview

1. Send a thank-you note or letter to the person you interviewed. If you don't know how to write one, ask your teacher or parent to help you.
2. Return any equipment that you checked out or borrowed.
3. If you did not tape the interview, check your notes *immediately after the interview* to write down anything you didn't have time to write during the interview. It's important to finish writing notes immediately after the interview, or you will forget what the person said. You may not forget everything, but you could forget some important details.

Privacy and *informed consent* are two related issues that you must consider in all interviews. First, the person you are interviewing may not wish to be identified in any way. You must obtain the person's permission to identify him or her. If the person wants his or her identity to be protected, you can still report information from the interview. To protect the person's identity, simply say that the answers came from a "seventeen-year-old" or some other description that tells your audience about the person without giving the identity away.

Second, if you use a video- or audiotape of the interview, make sure that you have obtained permission from the person. Never hide a camera or tape recorder!

FIGURE 5.4   Interview guide handout for students.

checked in advance, students will be protected as they make fruitful electronic searches for informants.

New search engines that are hitting the market help students to find web sites. Web Compass, by Quarterdeck, for example, finds web sites related to particular keywords. The program does the search overnight, so when you return to school or to your computer in the morning, a library of sites is waiting. The descriptions of each site give a good indication of the quality and content of the site and tell whether images and graphics reside at the site. Another particularly useful feature is that the program indicates whether the site is linked to other sites that may be useful.

Of course, this is just a single scratch on the surface of what can be found on the web.

Step 5: Taking Notes

As students found information, they took notes. The K-W-L format provided a three-column note-taking guide as students would write down what they had learned about their various "want to know" questions. We sometimes had students use power outlining, in which they classified levels of information from most general to most specific, and traditional kinds of note cards.

We modeled various ways of taking notes that mirrored work that we did throughout the year on reading for key details and main ideas. Students were guided to notice key details by paying attention to titles, paragraphing, markers such as boldface type and italics, graphics, text structure, transitions, surprises, and the like. The key details were notated in some way, through words or sometimes pictures. (For a full description of picture mapping, see Wilhelm 1997.) These key details were then analyzed to discern the central focus or main idea of the whole text.

Students often wanted to take notes, print, or copy information from the web or other electronic sources. The hypertextual environment provides different possibilities and challenges for students who are gleaning information from online sites. We prohibited students from printing multiple screens from web sites, but did allow them to copy and paste particular images or sections into a notebook word processing document. In our own opinion, this copy-paste mechanism didn't help students to own the information or be as critical about it as using some kind of notetaking chart (like K-W-L) or template. So even with web searches, students were encouraged to use charts or note cards as a way of recording important data.

Daily Planning and Reflection

In an extended project, it's important to keep track of student progress and to be accountable to each group and each student. It's also important for students to be accountable to their group, the class, and the teacher. To help us make our progress visible and our learning accountable, we had a variety of techniques that the students used daily to publicize where they were, what they had done, and what they were planning to do next. We had various procedures in place to make sure no one fell through the cracks. The students were responsible for demonstrating their progress through these techniques. It made our own progress checks quick and easy, and it helped us to know who needed help when. We were able to use our class time wisely to address general concerns or help individuals who most needed it without getting in the way of students who were doing nicely on their own.

Exit and Entrance Slips

To facilitate planning and reflection, students were asked to write quick *exit slips* that reported what they had done that day. Students handed these to us as they left the classroom as their "pass" out of the classroom. If we felt a particular student had not used her time wisely, we could converse with her as she departed. This also helped students to self-monitor their daily progress and provided daily feedback to us of how things were going.

Students would then gain entry into class the next day with a quick *entrance slip* that outlined their plans for the day. In this way, each student had committed to a daily plan. This helped students to get to work quickly and helped us to know what they were doing and anticipate how they might need help.

At the beginning of the project, we might provide students with exit slips with blank spaces for their name, their achievements during class time, and how they could demonstrate this achievement. As the project progressed, students would write their own exit and entrance slips on notebook paper. Such slips took only a minute to write, helped students reflect on what they had done and needed to do, and served as signposts to us of where they were in terms of the project. These slips would only take a moment to flip through.

Reflective Journals

Once or twice a week, students composed slightly lengthier reflective journal entries recording where they were, what had gone well, how and why they had made decisions, what they needed to do next, and what kind of help they anticipated needing from peers or the teachers. Questions could be asked and frustrations vented.

Design Diaries

Later in the project, once students were working on the computer, they created *design diaries,* which were hidden in their hyperstacks (Lehrer 1993). These diaries were essentially pop-up fields, which they used to record what had been done and to justify their work and progress at the end of each class. This work substituted for exit slips; students would leave their diary on the screen as we walked around to check them before dismissal from class.

These techniques took only a little bit of time, but structured an element of continual reflection into the project. Students learned to monitor what they had done and needed to do next, and to become critical about the processes and products of their learning (Erickson 1997; Lehrer et al. 1994). Various research, such as that by Edmiston (1991), has shown that reflection is a necessary component of learning, and particularly of gaining metacognitive control over one's own learning processes.

Keeping Track and Keeping on Track

Students were collecting a tremendous amount of data from a wide variety of sources. (We will explore how to organize these data in Chapter 6.) As their teachers, we had 130 students to keep track of who were all doing different things, were experiencing different problems, and were at different places in their progress. We needed to provide quick and efficient ways to assist students in keeping track of the information they had gleaned, plus where they were, what they had done, and what they still needed to do. As teachers, we too needed to have ways to keep track of student work and to know when to provide interventions such as minilessons, conferences, and other kinds of extra help. The strategies we have already listed helped us all to keep track of work on a daily basis. The following strategies helped us to keep track of where we were in terms of the total project.

Project Task Checklist

We tried to help students by providing a checklist of requirements and duties for each group (see Figure 5.5). But we found after the first year that this checksheet was too overwhelming for students to receive all at one time, so we divided the project into phases. Each group would receive a checklist for the phase of the project they were entering, such as Asking Questions/Finding Information. The phases all corresponded to aspects of the student design framework.

Each item on the checklist corresponded to a task that had to be completed. When the task was completed, individual students had to find both a peer who would initial that they had completed the task and then a teacher who would agree and then initial that they had completed the task. Needing to get peer approval before approaching the teacher with a completed task made students answerable to each other and helped screen us from truly incomplete or indefensible work. When shoddy work did reach us, we held both the perpetrator and the student who had initialed their work responsible.

When the entire phase was complete (as opposed to individual tasks in the phase) two teachers had to initial off (in our case this could be Paul; Jeff; Judy, our learning specialist; Pat, our English teacher; the librarian; or a student teacher who might be working with us). The student was then free to enter the next phase of the project. She would get a new sheet and earn new privileges associated with the next phase, such as going to the library to find information as opposed to staying in the classroom to continue refining research questions, or being able to spend time on a computer after demonstrating that she had something to design through planning sheets and design proposals. The checksheets helped both students and teachers monitor progress. The privileges that accrued in each phase, particularly that of gaining access to computers, provided plenty of motivation for students to complete efficient and high-quality work on previous phases.

Another benefit was that students would not find themselves in the computer lab or at another learning station unless they had demonstrated that they were ready to be there and could take advantage of being there. This saved valuable computer time from being wasted. Our school had

Cultural Journalism Hypercard Project

Phase 1: Asking Questions/Finding Information
_____ 1. Topic _____
_____ 2. Related questions (brainstorming)
_____ 3. Subtopics
_____ 4. Related questions (brainstorming)
_____ 5. Initial bibliography (sources) # _____

Phase 2: Organize/Add Information
_____ 1. Initial plan tree
_____ 2. Notes on subtopics
_____ 3. Add to bibliography # _____
_____ 4. Schedule interview (Person: _____ Date: _____)
_____ 5. Develop interview questions
_____ 6. Conduct interview
_____ 7. Discuss topics with group

Phase 3: Add/Analyze/Reorganize
_____ 1. Read secondary sources (stories, myths, travel brochures, etc.)
         Titles: _____
_____ 2. Revised plan tree
_____ 3. List other sources of information
         Food _____
         Video _____
         Music _____
         Clothing _____
         Artifacts _____
_____ 4. Submit bibliography
_____ 5. Web with cross-links to group members' topics
_____ 6. Peer review of cards

Phase 4: Card/Stack Design
_____ 1. Design diary
_____ 2. Main menu card
_____   Background _____ Buttons _____ Links _____ Pictures/sound
_____ 3. _Subtopic 1_ main menu card _____
_____   Text _____ Background _____ Buttons _____ Links _____ Pictures/sound
_____ 4. Subtopic supporting detail _____
_____   Text _____ Background _____ Buttons _____ Links _____ Pictures/sound
_____ 4. Subtopic supporting detail _____
_____   Text _____ Background _____ Buttons _____ Links _____ Pictures/sound
_____ 4. Subtopic supporting detail _____
_____   Text _____ Background _____ Buttons _____ Links _____ Pictures/sound

FIGURE 5.5   Checklist of requirements and duties for each group.

Cultural Journalism Hypercard Project

_____ 3. *Subtopic 2* main menu card _____				
_____ Text ____ Background _____	Buttons _____	Links ____	Pictures/sound
_____ 4. Subtopic supporting detail _____				
_____ Text ____ Background _____	Buttons _____	Links ____	Pictures/sound
_____ 4. Subtopic supporting detail _____				
_____ Text ____ Background _____	Buttons _____	Links ____	Pictures/sound
_____ 4. Subtopic supporting detail _____				
_____ Text ____ Background _____	Buttons _____	Links ____	Pictures/sound
_____ 3. *Subtopic 3* main menu card _____				
_____ Text ____ Background _____	Buttons _____	Links ____	Pictures/sound
_____ 4. Subtopic supporting detail _____				
_____ Text ____ Background _____	Buttons _____	Links ____	Pictures/sound
_____ 4. Subtopic supporting detail _____				
_____ Text ____ Background _____	Buttons _____	Links ____	Pictures/sound
_____ 4. Subtopic supporting detail _____				
_____ Text ____ Background _____	Buttons _____	Links ____	Pictures/sound
_____ 3. *Subtopic 4* main menu card _____				
_____ Text ____ Background _____	Buttons _____	Links ____	Pictures/sound
_____ 4. Subtopic supporting detail _____				
_____ Text ____ Background _____	Buttons _____	Links ____	Pictures/sound
_____ 4. Subtopic supporting detail _____				
_____ Text ____ Background _____	Buttons _____	Links ____	Pictures/sound
_____ 4. Subtopic supporting detail _____				
_____ Text ____ Background _____	Buttons _____	Links ____	Pictures/sound
_____ 3. *Subtopic 5* main menu card _____				
_____ Text ____ Background _____	Buttons _____	Links ____	Pictures/sound
_____ 4. Subtopic supporting detail _____				
_____ Text ____ Background _____	Buttons _____	Links ____	Pictures/sound
_____ 4. Subtopic supporting detail _____				
_____ Text ____ Background _____	Buttons _____	Links ____	Pictures/sound
_____ 4. Subtopic supporting detail _____				
_____ Text ____ Background _____	Buttons _____	Links ____	Pictures/sound

FIGURE 5.5 **continued**

only one computer lab of Mac Classics, which we shared with six other houses, consisting of about six hundred other students. As a result, we had to do significant work off the computer (no problem—even professional multimedia designers do this) and use our scheduled computer time with maximum efficiency. That meant that anyone on a computer was prepared to do project work that could only be done on the computer.

Conferences

We informally conferenced with groups and individuals each day about their work. We also planned to have one of us conference with each group each week to review how they were doing and what they needed to do next.

This conferencing was not as difficult as it might sound. Although there were groups who needed guidance, once we got going with the project, most students had a clear agenda that they pursued on their own. As teachers, we always had time to walk around the classroom or lab, checking in and talking to students about their work, answering questions that came up, and providing on-the-spot advice. By planning one formal group conference a day for each class period, we could conference with each group once a week. These meetings took five minutes and gave us the rest of class time for mini-lessons and informal types of conferences and situated teaching.

Teaching Strategies

The checklists, both planned and unplanned daily conferences, and the continual feedback we received from the slips, journals, and student work helped us monitor student progress. The checklists in particular required the students to share their work regularly and receive feedback on it from both peers and teachers.

We, as teaching teammates, also informally conferenced together several times during the day—as we worked together, or in the hallways between classes when we were working in different spaces or learning stations. We made a habit of writing down observations, particularly about perceived problems and concerns. We could then converse about these issues and brainstorm solutions after school, often working overnight on mini-lessons or making plans to conference with particular students.

We worked with several other teachers as part of our team and had team planning time scheduled into our day. Since not all of our team members were involved in our project (though we increasingly involved them over the years), we often used two of our team planning periods a week to work on our project with those who were involved. The other three days were devoted to issues and discussions concerning team issues or secretarial duties that did not impinge on our actual teaching of the unit.

This kind of teaching was easier in many ways than our more

traditional teaching. Students were generally much more motivated and took charge of their own learning to a greater extent. Although keeping track of their progress took energy, we did not have the daily grind of formal lesson plans or sets of quizzes, papers, and tests. Instead, we were continually monitoring student progress on their extended project and providing instruction at the point of need, which made such instruction more accessible and important to the students. Much responsibility was given to the students to approach us for feedback and to make sure to demonstrate that they were on track. We constantly reinforced to the students that they needed to "make their learning visible!" (Brown and Campione 1996; Erickson 1997; Erickson and Lehrer, in press). The proof of learning was in the pudding of their process, and of their product of a completed hyperstack.

Chapter 6

Dealing with Information

Important Points

This chapter describes how students were taught to categorize, classify, chunk, and organize their information to make it ready to be entered on hypercards. The process of using pyramids, issue trees, and webs to organize information is explained in detail. The chapter concludes with an explanation of how to prompt students to generate cross-links (associative links) within their own and between group members' stacks.

➥ Information is not knowledge until it is organized, systematic, extensible, and usable.

➥ Adolescents are not good organizers by nature. They need to be taught how to organize information and structure knowledge.

➥ Integrating the curriculum and dividing teaching responsibilities enhances instruction and learning.

➥ Pyramids help students organize information.

➥ Issue trees and webs allow for identifying cross-links, which are associative links between separate categories.

➥ Issue trees and webs of information make it easier to move to hypermedia computer organization.

The value of information about information can be greater than the value of the information itself.

Negroponte (1995, p. 154)

Robby: Man, I know so much stuff now. I know piles of stuff. There is no way I can put all this in my stack!
Dr. J: That's good. If you put it all in there no one would read it. Most readers won't read your whole hyperstack anyway, but only the parts that really grab them. What you need to do now is to figure out what is really important and only keep that. Then provide your readers with a menu, titles and headers so they will know which cards they want to read and be directed to them.

Classroom exchange, late February 1994

Over the Finding Information phase of the unit, our students had collected and digested a great deal of information. But information, though necessary, is not a sufficient condition for carrying out inquiry to its satisfactory conclusion. Information is not knowledge. At this point, our students had gathered and read data relevant to their questions from a wide variety of electronic and nonelectronic sources. They had learned what makes a good research question, how to find information in the real world (e.g., from embassies, real-world informants, artifacts), how to interview someone, and how to take notes in different ways. They had done prodigious and intense work collecting and comprehending data. Now loomed the task of synthesizing and communicating it to others.

Information is not knowledge until it is organized, systematic, extensible, and usable (Perkins 1986). We believe that the data must be patterned, linked, and related to other ideas so that what is known is contextualized. Coherence requires sensible patterning and elaboration. Knowledge should be something that can be understood, extended, and added to by others, and it must be accessible and applicable by these others. Nicholas Negroponte (1995) has argued that intelligence lies in interconnection and that knowledge is something extensible about which the audience will ask, "Tell me more!"

In order to help our students transform the raw data and cook it into a flavorful, fully interpreted meal, it had to be made ordered and fulfilling.

To help this come about, we had to do considerable work to help our students see the patterns in their data, select that which was important and discard what wasn't, and begin organizing what was important into a system that could be understood and built upon (Lehrer 1993; Lehrer et al. 1994). To do this, we used three techniques that built successively on each other: pyramiding, issue treeing, and webbing.

All three techniques helped students to categorize separate pieces of data together and see relationships among different chunks or piles of information and how these relationships contributed to the meaning of a whole text. We called this chunking *classification.* We repeatedly reminded the students that all thought depends on generalizing and seeing patterns. In reading classes, we would ask things like, "How do we know a round thing is a ball, a piece of fruit, or a circle unless we can classify things into groups?" We repeatedly focused on this classification scheme, which we put on a poster and liked to chant:

- Identify a Universe! (Choose a definable topic for your question.)
- Define a Basis! (Decide how you will define and divide ideas into subtopics based on particular criteria.)
- Coordinate! (Put separate ideas of equal importance or value on the same level of your pyramid or tree.)
- Subordinate! (Make sure you have specific key details that fit under each subtopic.)

Pyramids

At the completion of the Finding Information phase, students had collected well-cited quotes, notes, and summaries. Each of these information chunks represented a possibly pivotal piece in completing a much larger puzzle. The goal of this puzzle was to piece together a document that would answer each student's research question and contribute to answering the group's broader question. The key was putting the puzzle together in a sensible, coherent, and thorough way. To do this, we needed to guide students through the process of organizing their information.

We started this process in reading classes. The first organizational tool we used was a *pyramid,* a tool that relates information hierarchically, as in Figure 6.1. We started with a pyramid because the shape allowed students to see the process of building an argument in an architectural way. Students had already used pyramids to represent the organization

Religion of
the Blackfoot

The Blackfoot were much more
religious and considerate of
nature than most people are today.

Teaching	Dances	Ceremonies	Religious Objects	Important People and Roles	Worship
family watching effect of environment	Ghost Dance Black-tailed Deer Dance Sun Dance Dance for the spirits of the dead Stick game dance	Feasts Vision Quest All-smoking ceremony Marrige	Lizard Charm Medicine bundle Pipes Eagle feathers Quillwork	Medicine men + women Chiefs Warriors	Meditation Creator spirits missionaries creation story

FIGURE 6.1   A student-created pyramid of researched information.

of a few of the books or articles they had read in reading class. The pyramid allowed us to show the various ways in which both narrative and expository texts were constructed, organized, and developed. The pyramid made the organization of a piece transparent, and showed how the parts of a text are related and contribute to the total effect and point, or main idea, which we called a *central focus.* Cause and effect, pro and con, classification, and narratives were just a few of the kinds of textual organization with which a pyramid worked successfully. Therefore, students had a context for the use of the pyramid upon which they could draw both familiarity and comfort.

In our lessons, we worked to create an understanding of how information can be organized. The pyramid proved to be an effective way of demonstrating that you didn't just give the answer to a research question. A well-written research text should provide facts, details, explanations, and stories to support and provide evidence for the answer to a question. If they had done the requisite research, their answers might be very complex and involve some kind of argument, such as, "We know this is a possible answer to our question because . . ."

We emphasized to students that they would need to do something with their data, as opposed to just listing or presenting the information. They would need to contextualize the data, organize them, and explain how different chunks worked to answer the research question. (For a useful discussion of teaching argument, see Hillocks 1995.)

The pyramid helped the students begin to divide and categorize the information they had collected. They began determining how each piece of information was going to help provide evidence for and tell the story that would provide a complete answer to their overall research question.

We worked to help students identify why they thought the facts they had gathered were reliable and to identify what work the facts did to answer their questions. Students in an electronic age must constantly ask: "How do I know what I know? How do I know that what I know is really true?" A brief foray into the Internet will demonstrate how important this categorically tentative stance toward "facts" has become since anyone can publish, or "post," anything. In contrast to books such as this one, where editors and publishers employ experts from the field to review and confirm the reliability and correctness of information, no such cautions are required for Internet publishing. We tried to help our students to examine and establish such criteria and "critical stances" toward their work and to understand that all facts, even scientific ones, have been socially constructed and are therefore open to scrutiny and debate.

Meeting the Challenge

For some students, organizing the information they had collected and framing it into an organized argument proved to be a real challenge. In social studies class one day as we began the Analyzing and Organizing Phase of the project, I (Paul) could tell that Andy was less than enthusiastic. His facial expression alone expressed profound disagreement with me. His hand held high signaled that its owner was awaiting permission to offer a challenge. I called on Andy, accepting his challenge. He said in utter dismay, "You mean getting all this information wasn't good enough? Now I have to organize it?"

My response was, "What good is your information unless it is organized? Will I know the answer to your research question if you just hand in your research notes?"

Andy thought for a moment and said, "Yeah! You're a smart teacher. You'll be able to get it."

I thanked Andy for his great confidence in my abilities but then explained that I was not the only audience for his project and that it would be very difficult for me or anyone else to make sense of his notes in their current form. I probably could do it, but only with much difficulty. I told Andy that *he* was the expert. He knew the context of his research puzzle process and could therefore put the material together and organize it much better and with more ease than I could.

Andy liked being called an expert, so he relaxed a bit. His posture and countenance told me that he would listen to what I was going to say. The rest of the class followed his lead. I continued with my instruction, confident that I had their attention—for the moment.

I used the chalkboard to show the students how I might organize information collected on the topic of religion—the topic Andy had chosen to cover as part of his group's work to analyze and explain the culture of the Iroquois Indians.

We liked to use student work as the basis of our examples of how to do different parts of the project. It ensured that our example would be appropriate to what our students understood and were next ready to learn. Students also seem to be more interested in looking at other students' work, so they were more engaged in the learning.

I told Andy that I would need his expert help to complete my example. Andy, now suddenly serious and very involved, nodded to affirm his readiness. I began the process by filling in the top of the pyramid with Andy's topic, "Iroquois Religion." Next, I asked Andy what his central focus or main research question was. Andy told me that he was looking at why and how religion was important to the Iroquois. I filled this information in the second box from the top of the pyramid.

Then I said, "Now comes the fun part."

Andy smiled and asked, "What do you mean?"

"Well, now is where we have to start organizing our information."

As Andy started to fidget just a bit, I asked him to think about the information he had gathered on religion, the question web he had constructed, and the attributes of religion within a culture that we had studied a few weeks ago. I asked him to determine if there were any subtopics that we could break his information into. Andy looked at this information in his notebook and then back at me, then at his notebook again, then his classmates. Then his face colored a bit, and he said, "I don't get it!"

I was prepared for this answer because we had found that seventh-grade students couldn't organize their own locker, much less something as abstract and complex as information. I tried again, this time asking Andy to start telling me about what he had found in his research of religion. Andy quickly obliged; this was something he could do. As he read through the information, I asked the class to help us by suggesting any common themes or subtopics that seemed to develop.

Organizational activities such as this are one of the real strengths of learning through the use of hypermedia. Students are often asked to tell all the information they know about something ("Knowledge Telling" in writing; Scardamalia and Bereiter 1992; Hayes and Flower 1980) in the form of an essay or book report. Seldom in school are students required to analyze, organize, or transform information. If students are to be able to do this work, we must give them practice. I told the students they could think of it as a brainstorming activity. I felt that would release any reservations they may have had about volunteering subtopics in front of the class. But Andy didn't get very far, and hands started to go up around the room.

I pointed at Jenny and asked, "Jenny, what do you see?"

"Well, it seems like he is mentioning the word *ceremony* a lot," Jenny answered.

"Good observation. I'm going to write 'ceremonies' down as a subtopic in the pyramid," I replied.

Brad, next to volunteer, stated, "It seems like Andy has a lot of information on dances they did as part of their religion. Shouldn't we have a subtopic on that?"

I nodded my head and smiled. "Absolutely!" I said in quick agreement. I wrote the word *dances* in the next box in the pyramid.

Andy now had his hand up, so I called on him.

"I think I see how it works. We're putting things that are the same together and giving them a title," he reflected.

Andy was right. We had been identifying themes and categorizing data. The stacked-up pieces of information should eventually build a pyramid that would provide an answer to the students' research question.

"Yes, that is a good description of what we are doing," I answered.

The class was really on top of it now. I drew on their energy, and we continued to fill in our pyramid with subtopics for the information that Andy had collected. Then, just as quick as the energy formed, it began to wane. We sat in silence for a few minutes looking at the pyramid (see Figure 6.2). I asked the students if they were satisfied with the subtopics. Most students seemed to nod that they were, but Andy did not seem convinced. He had his hand in the air again and a worried look on his face.

"What's wrong, Andy?" I asked.

"How do I know if this pyramid is right? I mean, is this good enough?"

I smiled and said, "Andy you are once again showing us your expertise. We must all ask ourselves the question that you ask. The answer will come in our next step. It is time to put the actual information that we have collected into our pyramid under our subtopic headings."

FIGURE 6.2   Andy's pyramid with subtopics as completed by the class.

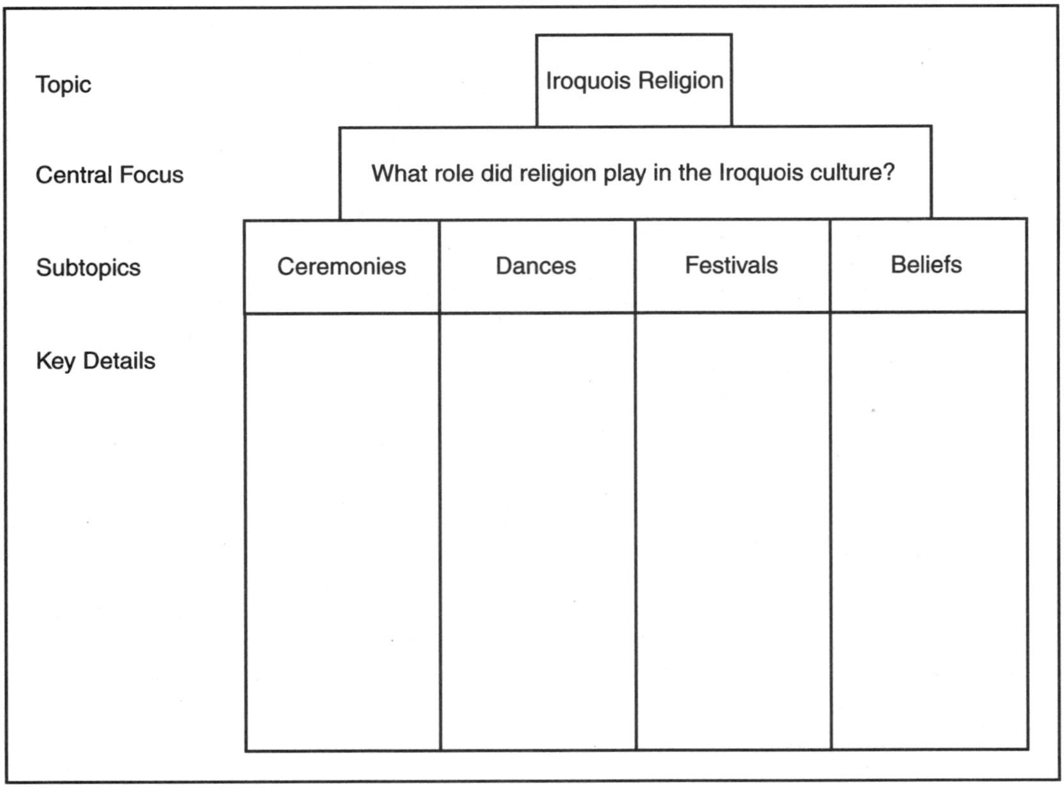

Topic		Iroquois Religion		
Central Focus		What role did religion play in the Iroquois culture?		
Subtopics	Ceremonies	Dances	Festivals	Beliefs
Key Details				

Andy was once again confident. "That's going to be easy. We made our subtopics based on research notes, so I know where the information fits in," he said.

"You should be right, Andy," I agreed. "The actual details from your research notes should plug into the subtopics nicely."

I drew boxes under the subtopics in our pyramid to fill in the base. I asked Andy to read his research notes to us once again so we could work together to put them under the correct subtopics. As we worked, I told students that I was going to jot down keywords from Andy's research notes. That way, we could note the information and also save room for other pieces of information. I suggested to Andy that he circle the keyword in each of his research notes or write in the margin so that he would remember what each keyword meant.

We worked our way through Andy's research. I continued to reinforce our goal and strategy by repeatedly asking for the correct category for a piece of data such as subtopic or key detail. Soon we had all his information noted in the pyramid. We all reflected on our masterpiece for a moment, catching our breath—or at least I was catching mine!—I turned to the class and said, "Now it's time to think about the question that Andy asked earlier. Is this good enough?"

The class sat silently staring at the pyramid (see Figure 6.3). I didn't need ESP to figure out that most of the class was hoping that what we had was indeed good enough. Andy was certainly part of this group. I shifted my focus to Andy again, asking him if he thought this was good enough. Andy thought for a second and then shrugged.

I returned my focus to the class: "When we ask if this is good enough, we are really asking if this information is good enough to do what?"

Again the class sat silently, but I wasn't going to save them this time. They sat looking at the pyramid and I at them. My room was quiet enough to hear the wheels grinding in their heads as they struggled to find the answer. It was Andy who had the light bulb go on first. He didn't bother raising his hand. His eyes just opened wide and he blurted, "To answer my question!" Then he looked at me and explained, "I mean, my information needs to answer the question at the top of my pyramid."

I smiled and replied, "Exactly, Andy. If your information and subtopics don't answer the question that you set out to answer, then something has to happen. Either we must go back and figure out what else we need to find to answer our question, or we must revise our research question."

I explained that a research question gets revised only if the information found clearly shows that a change of focus is needed. I said that this does

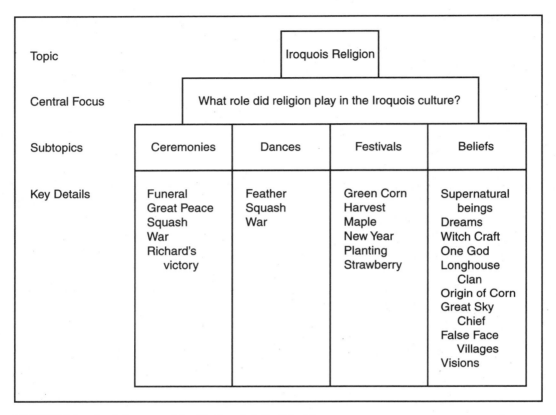

Topic		Iroquois Religion		
Central Focus		What role did religion play in the Iroquois culture?		
Subtopics	Ceremonies	Dances	Festivals	Beliefs

Key Details	Funeral
	Great Peace
	Squash
	War
	Richard's
	    victory
		Feather
		Squash
		War
			Green Corn
			Harvest
			Maple
			New Year
			Planting
			Strawberry
				Supernatural
				    beings
				Dreams
				Witch Craft
				One God
				Longhouse
				    Clan
				Origin of Corn
				Great Sky
				    Chief
				False Face
				    Villages
				Visions

FIGURE 6.3   Andy's pyramid with the details filled in.

happen sometimes, but that more often, you find that you need to find answers to new questions that you have based on an analysis of the information you have already found.

I looked back at Andy. "Andy you're the expert. Have you answered your question?"

Andy looked at the pyramid for a few moments and said, "Yeah, I think I have."

I could tell by the way he emphasized the first "I" that his response was both an answer and a question. Andy really wanted to know what I thought. I smiled at Andy and turned to the class and asked them to look at the pyramid. I reminded them that the base of a pyramid had to be very strong and wide to stabilize and hold up the entire pyramid. To support the pyramid, the base had to be composed of the key details, and specific examples, stories, pictures, explanations, and other artifacts that addressed and helped to answer their research question. It was important for their whole group to work together and make sure that the pyramids of all the group's members were strong and clearly provided the details that answered each research question and in some way helped to answer the group's general question.

At this point, another boy in the class asked, "But what about coverage? I mean, don't you have to have covered all the important information that would answer your question?"

"Good point!" I agreed. "Thoroughness would be another important quality of a good pyramid. Though I doubt you would ever find all the important information that would help answer your question, you should make the effort to be thorough and provide your audience with the most important available information that works to answer your research question."

We gave the students time to work on their pyramids and discuss them in their groups in a roundtable session. On the due date, we checked each pyramid and wrote suggestions and comments, then gave students an opportunity to reflect and revise. Students made necessary additions and changes. Not until a student's pyramid was acceptable to the author, the group, and us did we initial this item on their project checklist to verify its completion. Now the students were ready to learn additional tools for organizing information, the next step in the project.

Issue Trees and Webs

The next step in our project was to have students organize their information in a less linear form. This was important for several reasons. First, students need to learn several forms of organization so that they find the one that works best for them on future projects. Second, reorganizing the information often helps students to understand the information better and make it more systematic, extensible, and usable. Finally, reorganizing the information in a less linear way is more conducive to encouraging hypermedia document construction. The pyramid represented a fairly rigid and linear organization. It was time to move the students toward an organization that would be more similar to the flexible and nonlinear setup of a hypermedia document.

We chose a type of graphic organizer that we referred to as an *issue tree,* which could easily be made into a web by connecting the subtopics (see Figure 6.4). Any graphic organizer that allows you to spread your information out and show the various interconnections among different pieces will serve the purpose of this activity.

At this point in the project, students need to have a general understanding of how a hypermedia document works. We had made the hypermedia software familiar and accessible to students through two previous small-scale projects—the personality profile and psychology stack. If we had not done this, now would be the time to take a break from the information and teach the students how the program works.

Students do not need to master the program. They need only to be familiar with how the software operates and how hypermedia documents are structured. Guiding students through the creation of a very small practice stack, as described in Chapter 2, would work nicely at this point.

FIGURE 6.4   Example of an issue tree/web.

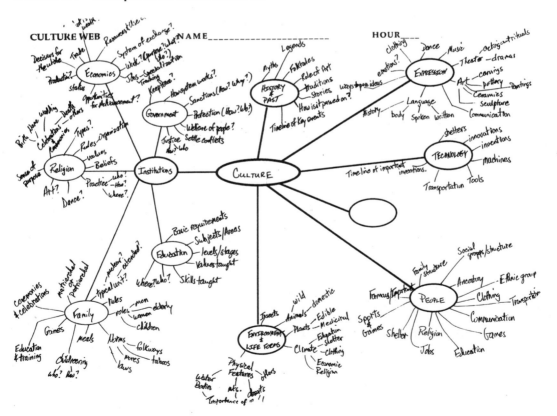

Since our students had this familiarity already, I built on what they already knew and connected hypermedia to the new organization tools. I reminded the class that the nature of hypermedia is that one piece of information can be connected or linked to many other related pieces of information. Our pyramid was too rigid to allow us to do that, so in order to make good hypermedia stacks, we would need to reorganize the information in a less rigid way. To do this, we would use issue trees and webs.

An *issue tree* is a graphic organizer. The main idea or central focus is put at the top and represents the roots and main trunk. The tree then grows upside down. Each subtopic is a branch of the tree, and the key details are the smaller branches off each main branch. Where the pyramid helps the students understand how they "build" support for their solution or argument, the tree has the branching quality that helps students begin to understand the idea of linking or connecting ideas and information.

The linking concept is very important to hypermedia. In every hypermedia document, screens or cards are linked together in various ways. A web is much like a tree except a web features many cross-links or associative links, where one category may have links across to other categories. Some projects or topics have more reason for the cross-links than others.

I told students that the good news was that it would not be as hard as the first time they organized their information into pyramids. The bad news was they had to do it in order to get to the next step of designing stack and card plans. Andy rolled his eyes.

To teach the process of translating the pyramid into an issue tree, I started with something we were all familiar with: the pyramid that we made together based on Andy's information. I displayed Andy's pyramid and told everyone to create the issue tree along with me in their notebooks, so they would have an example to work from when they did the reorganization on their own.

Jenny asked me, "Why do you keep calling it both a web and a tree? It can't be both, can it?"

"That's a good question, Jenny," I responded. "In our case, it is a tree *and* a web. It will look like a tree in that it will have main branches that attach to small branches. It will also look like a web in that some of those branches will attach to each other."

Jenny cut in. "If the branches attach to each other, then it's not a tree," she said in a "ha-ha I showed you wrong" voice.

I smiled, nodded, and agreed, saying, "You're right; it's not a tree." Jenny sat taller in her seat quite happy with herself. "But," I added, "it is not a web either." Jenny frowned, but before she could say anything, I cut her off with a question. "Jenny have you ever seen a spider's web that didn't connect all the way around it?"

She thought for a moment. "No, I guess not."

My case was almost won. "That is why I say we are making both a tree and web combined. It branches like a tree, but everything does not connect to everything else. We may have only a few of those weblike crosslinks [links that make a semantic connection to separate branches or topics within a web or tree as opposed to links that connect within the same branch from topics to subtopics to key details] in our computer document. So we are both right."

Jenny was happy that she was at least partially right. I was able to move on reasonably assured that my students understood. I began again, at the top of Andy's pyramid. I wrote down Andy's topic and research question together at the top of my work space. I explained to the class that this was the trunk of our tree. I also pointed out that our tree would be growing upside down. I feared another adversarial battle with Jenny, but she let it go.

Next, I branched off the subtopics. I described these as the main branches of our tree. I reminded students that each tree could have a different number of branches because they were all unique. The last step was to make smaller branches off the subtopics, which were the key details from the pyramid. Again, I stressed to students that they could put down keywords and phrases instead of the full text of their research notes. When we finished this step, we had a fine-looking upside-down tree.

Jenny spotted this right away. "See that's a tree, not a web," she bragged.

"Yes. So far it only resembles a tree. Our next job is to look for those other connections that make it more like a web," I replied.

I continued by explaining to the class that we could connect things within this tree that were related. By making these connections, we could show our audience how things fit together and are related. If we did a good job, our audience would come away with a better understanding of what we were trying to teach them. Andy had his hand up, so I called on him.

"I think I actually understand this time. If you look at my tree . . ." He hesitated before continuing. "Can I get up and show you?" He asked.

"Sure!" I replied.

He moved to the front of the room and continued. "If you look at my tree, you can see that I have information on a religious ceremony called the war ceremony, and in my dances subtopic I have information on the war dance. Some of the dances are dances that are part of a religious ceremony. So I could draw a branch or line over to dances from ceremonies because they are related." (See Figure 6.5.)

After I picked up my jaw, I clapped and said, "Bravo! I could not have said that better myself." Andy took a few bows for the class, put the chalk down, and went back to his seat. We worked as a class to find more of these cross-links, or associative relationships. The addition of each new cross-link made Andy's tree look more and more like a web.

The students were given the assignment of reorganizing their pyramids in this way. On the due date, Jeff and I checked their issue trees and again wrote comments and suggestions and discussed them with the students. This was another opportunity for students and teachers to look for gaps in

FIGURE 6.5 Andy's tree with the cross-links he describes drawn in.

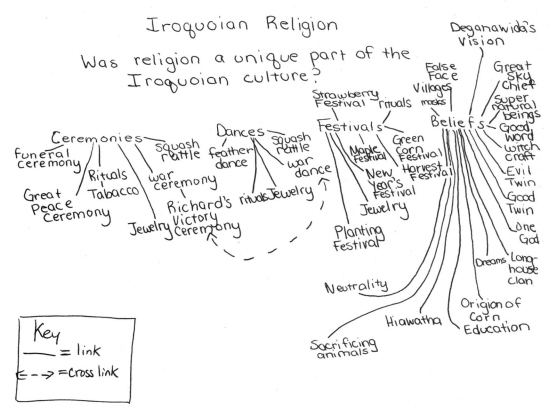

information and fill them in. We explained and demonstrated to our students that they had a gap in their tree or web if the information did not provide enough proof of their argument or adequately answer the sub-questions within their larger central focus question. We again made use of the project checksheet by initialing the tree as completed.

Most students had included some of the intraconnections or cross-links within their documents where they were warranted. There were a few students who tried to connect everything. Our usual strategy in these cases was to ask the students to explain how the pieces of information were related. Through one-on-one and whole-class discussions, our students came to a common understanding, or critical standard, of when it was proper to do this "cross-linking" within their stacks.

I sat next to Sarah, and we looked at the cross-links she had drawn in on her issue tree of the Iroquois Indians. She had drawn in cross-links virtually everywhere she had space on her paper.

"I see that you have connected everything in your tree to everything else, Sarah," I stated.

"Yeah, now it's a web," she replied.

"Is a web better than a tree?" I asked.

"Sure. Now I have a lot of those cross-links, so my information is all connected," Sarah answered.

"I think we need to review the reason behind making those connections or cross-links, Sarah," I stated.

Sarah and I went back over why we cross-link. Eventually she remembered that we draw cross-links between pieces of information that build on each other, provide for more example and proof, or generally help an audience better understand our information. For instance, Sarah had an excellent cross-link between information on religion and education. Her reason for making this link showed real insight: "I linked religion and education because the corn ceremony was religious but also was like a play of how they planted and took care of their corn, so it was also an educational ceremony." Sarah laughed after explaining the cross-link to me. "I guess I really didn't have any reason for most of those other cross-links I drew in. I just thought it would be better if everything was connected," she reflected.

I was finally comfortable believing that Sarah understood that connecting everything would probably be more confusing than enlightening. People who browsed her stack would be bounced around without any real connection to meaning. Conversely, the well-reasoned and justified cross-links she had created would help build understanding of her information and research argument.

As we discussed the issue trees, we both came to the realization that someone else might be able to start with the issue trees and skip the pyramid step. The pyramids were a good transition for our students, because it was a building-block organizational technique they were familiar and comfortable with.

We liked to wrap up this organization phase of our project with another roundtable discussion. Although some groups had a collaboratively authored piece to their document, all members of all groups also had an individual research question that related to and supported their group question. They therefore all had individual issue trees to plan out their individual stacks.

To help students see connections between their separate stacks and to reflect on their own information, we asked them to bring their individual trees to a roundtable. They laid all their individual trees down together so that everyone in the group could see them. At this point in the project, the groups were familiar with the information that each group member had collected. We were asking for a deeper look at the information this time. We wanted them to look for information in the other members' issue trees that related to something in their own.

We had students brainstorm all the possibilities and generate a list of possible intertree connections or cross-links between individuals' different hypermedia documents, creating a list of potential link candidates. Finally, the students made these connections on their trees with arrows to notations of where they possibly connected in another group member's tree.

They wrote the reason for each cross-link along the arrow that made the link. This helped students to reflect on and evaluate their list of link candidates. We collected and saved the lists for later in the project, when they would again be useful.

Students always seem to enjoy this activity. They learn even more about what each member of their group has found, and it draws the group closer. Their establishment of connections within the trees of the group seems to focus and bond the group in their goal to complete an integrated, collaborative project that depends on their weaving individual parts together into a coherent whole.

Chapter 7

Into the Lab: Designing Hyperstacks and

Creating Critical Scoring Guides

Important Points

This chapter explains the process of moving from issue trees and webs of information to creating the format of a hyperstack and creating actual hypercards. It explores the rewarding process of creating a scoring guide with students' input. The use of stack, subtopic, and individual card planning sheets is illustrated. The chapter demonstrates how designing on paper saves time in the computer lab and helps motivate students to work hard to get to the computer lab.

➥ Reflection on our learning and continual justification of what we were doing were of great importance in developing critical standards and producing high quality products (Erickson and Lehrer, in press).

➥ Students are required to demonstrate that they have done sufficient work to be allowed into the computer lab to work.

➥ Students will have more ownership in the criteria used to assess them if they have a hand in the creation of the criteria and the scoring guide. Such work helps students to articulate and apply their own critical standards, an important skill.

➥ Beware of students who get caught up by computer flash. They need to learn that various design features must serve the purpose of their document to communicate important understandings to their audience.

Knowledge itself results from and is a design.

D. N. Perkins (1986)

Making and seeing the scoring guide ahead of time was a good part of the project. It just seems so much more fair to know exactly what you're going to be graded on and to know that you agree with how you'll be graded.

Emily, seventh grader

Can we have a pass to the lab?

—A question posed to us repeatedly, usually by groups who wanted to get into the computer lab before school, during free periods and lunch, and particularly after school during the design phase of their projects

At the turn of this century, the educational philosopher John Dewey espoused learner-generated and teacher-guided educational projects built around efforts to combine purpose and structure. He advocated projects that would engage student interests, serve real human purposes, and could be used to achieve definable ends. The concept of design and the practice of designing has been identified as a natural, and ubiquitous, human activity (Norman 1988, cited by Lehrer et al. 1994).

Yet schools have not often considered how to encourage students to take on the role of designers in a classroom. As Rich Lehrer often told us, "Students are typically not enfranchised as designers." Both Rich and Julie have long argued that we must consider the advantages of putting students in this role and consider how best to help them to participate actively in design activities.

To be designers of hypermedia documents, students needed to have an idea of their ultimate purpose: Were they communicating to another seventh grader, an exchange student, or a businessperson, and for what reason? Thus, we asked students to articulate their intentions. Students also needed to understand how to create various kinds of artwork—video clips, graphics, sounds, animations, and written texts—since hypermedia allows them to author in multiple media forms. They could produce many of these things outside a computer environment and record or scan their products into the document. Yet many of these items could be created directly on the computer.

We are convinced that most of what can be learned by working on a computer can be learned through the planning, reading, reflection, and other activities that may best occur off a computer. In our classrooms, working on paper off the computer involved high levels of motivation and engaged learning by our students. Students wanted so much to get on the computers that they were willing to work hard and energetically to earn their right to get there.

For example, as students designed various audiovisuals and multimedia displays for their hyperstacks, they had to consider how each medium worked both alone and in conjunction with other media. They needed to know how to edit and segment visuals, such as video and audio sound, and learn how to "meld," or bring together, various media for particular effects. (For more on the potential for hypermedia and constructivist learning, see Lehrer, Erickson, and Connell 1994.)

We stressed that what was designed could not be pure flash or pyrotechnical displays of phantasmagoric multimedia expertise. Everything that was included in a stack had to contribute to the understanding and the experience of the audience. As students added both simple design features and sophisticated special effects to their work, we always asked: How does this help you make your point? Students demonstrated their motivation for completing the design phase of the project by going to the computer lab during lunch breaks, study halls, and even before and after school.

We also stressed using the expertise of each other to assist with content-area questions and with hypermedia design. In this way, distributed expertise was developed and spread throughout the school community (Brown and Campione 1994; Erickson 1997). Students would learn to design different kinds of effects, like animation or button iconography, and would then share that expertise with others, who would not have to learn the process from the ground up. Each student seemed to develop sophistication in different areas and in doing so became experts on different types of hypermedia programming or design.

As always, reflection on our learning and continual justification of what we were doing were of great importance in developing critical standards and producing high-quality products. We have found that when students are asked to explain why they are doing something in the design of their stack, it forces them to consider their audience and reflect on the purpose of their stack.

We often discussed individual examples with the whole class. This allowed us to keep fresh in the students' minds what makes a good hypermedia stack and what helps create understanding. Having students articulate their standards also exposes exactly what students know and don't know—critical in order to get them to where we wanted them to be. The discussions on standards and purpose acted as informal assessment tools and as a way of constantly nudging students to greater expertise.

These projects worked with nearly all of the struggling, at-risk, and labeled students we taught, including those labeled as cognitively disabled. We adapted the project to different students by asking how much assistance particular children needed to complete a project. With some of these students, we provided a blank hypermedia stack template that could be filled in, added to, or adapted. (Examples of blank stacks, student-made stacks, and other useful documents can be obtained at our web site for this book at www.nconnect.net/~frito.) With others, we provided more time for teacher or peer assistance. The point is that the project was challenging, and some children did struggle. But the platform of hypermedia and the process of constructivist teaching are both flexible and can be adapted to fit different needs.

Hyperlinks

Students were required to demonstrate that they had done sufficient work to be allowed into the computer lab to work (a motivator for kids who liked to work with computers or to program but weren't quite as thrilled with the preliminary research tasks). In order to gain an entrance ticket to the computer lab, students had to finish their issue trees and begin to plan their screen designs. These designs then had to demonstrate how they would communicate their information so that others could learn it.

We were satisfied with most of the issue trees that we evaluated. Jenny proudly held her checksheet over her head and declared that she had her "ticket" to the lab. I laughed and agreed that she was indeed close to making that trip, but there was still more preparation needed. Students had their issue trees and a basic idea of where they needed to go next. Since we were using HyperCard and HyperStudio to create the hypermedia documents, we referred to our documents as "stacks" and each screen as a "card." This terminology is the same or very similar in the dominant hypermedia software programs.

We came up with three hypermedia document planning sheets that would act as road maps so that all students had a greater chance of reaching their destination. We started with the stack plan sheet (see Figure 7.1). (You can obtain an electronic copy of this form and many others in this

STACK PLAN SHEET

NAME Holly Noe
HOUR 3
TRIBE Blackfoot
TOPIC Religion

Directions: Use this sheet to plan out the sub-topics you will break your topic/central focus into. The number of categories is up to you but the sub-topics should help to answer your central focus.

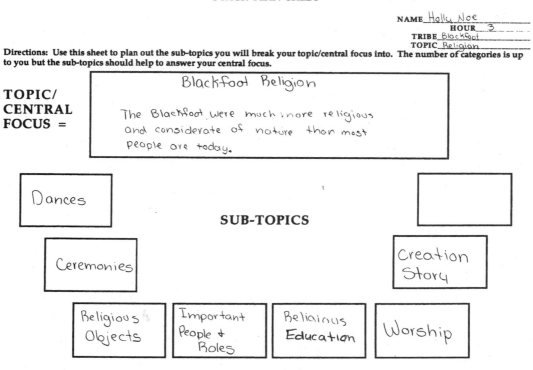

TOPIC/ CENTRAL FOCUS =

Blackfoot Religion

The Blackfoot were much more religious and considerate of nature than most people are today.

SUB-TOPICS

Dances

Ceremonies

Creation Story

Religious Objects

Important People & Roles

Religious Education

Worship

FIGURE 7.1   Stack plan sheet.

chapter at our web site.) Students use it to lay out their main menu to reflect on the overall organization of the stack and subtopic cards. The sheet also seemed to help students begin to think of how they would communicate their information in a hypermedia format and how their issue trees and webs translated into an organization on the computer.

The subtopic and card plan sheets followed. The subtopic plan sheet provided small card designing boxes that could be used to plan a subtopic of the student's issue tree. The card plan sheet was used to make detailed design plans for each individual card or screen.

Nicole asked, "Let me see if I've got this right? We start with a main menu or table of contents card, then make the subtopic cards, and last the key detail cards. Right?" This, in fact, reflected the organization of the issue trees the kids had created.

I (Paul) responded that yes, this was one way to do it but not the only way. The process could be done the other way around also, beginning with key detail or other particular cards. Many students raised an eyebrow at this revelation. I pointed out that what was really important was that they begin to think of and organize their information as separate cards that can be linked in any way they and their audience would see as meaningful. I reminded the students that they had drawn lines to connect information on their issue trees and that most of those connections would probably become links (reasons for buttons that connect those cards) within their hypermedia document.

We usually work through several examples of this metamorphosis with the students, using subjects that are familiar to most of the students, such as the organization of the NBA and NFL or the story map of a novel they had read in class. We are methodical about showing the students how the issue tree or web parts became cards in the plan sheets (see Figure 7.2). We always provide students with replicas of what we are doing on the overhead. They really appreciate the replicas and tell us they are helpful. Students seem to get a better understanding of the transformation process by working through examples using familiar information.

This model of teaching is similar to what Tharp and Gallimore (1990) call E-T-R. First, you elicit or provide student experience (E), then challenge it with disconfirming information, a problem to be solved, or some other kind of text (T) that will encourage a transformation of understanding or participation. What should result is a response (R) that demonstrates some kind of growth and new understanding.

At this point, most of the students were quite engaged in planning their hypermedia cards, and they were beginning to see what their stack might look like. My class was a scene of quiet, concentrating students working on their subtopic plan sheets (see Figure 7.3). Jake was the exception. He appeared to be talking to someone. I made my way over to Jake, hoping my close proximity would take care of the talking problem without disrupting the work of the rest of the class.

As I got closer to Jake, I realized that Jake was talking to himself! I was surprised; talking to oneself is usually not the stuff that "cool" is made of in the seventh grade. As I came up behind Jake, he still did not notice me. I watched with a silent smile as Jake continued to talk so that he could hear his own thoughts. As soon as his words were spoken, his pencil would fly on his paper, quickly recording each idea before it could dissipate into the air of the classroom.

My curiosity got the better of me, and I discreetly asked Jake how he was doing. Jake was startled by my voice and then smiled and said, "It makes sense now. I can see how it all fits together. I'm writing notes next

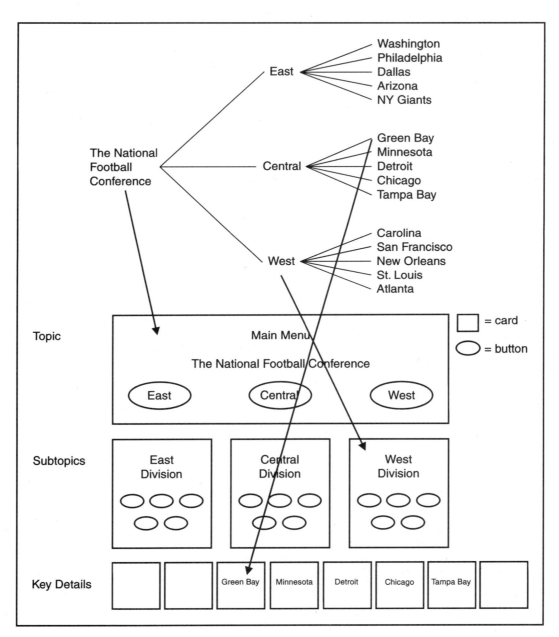

FIGURE 7.2 Example of a model to teach the transition from tree to web using the organization of the NFL.

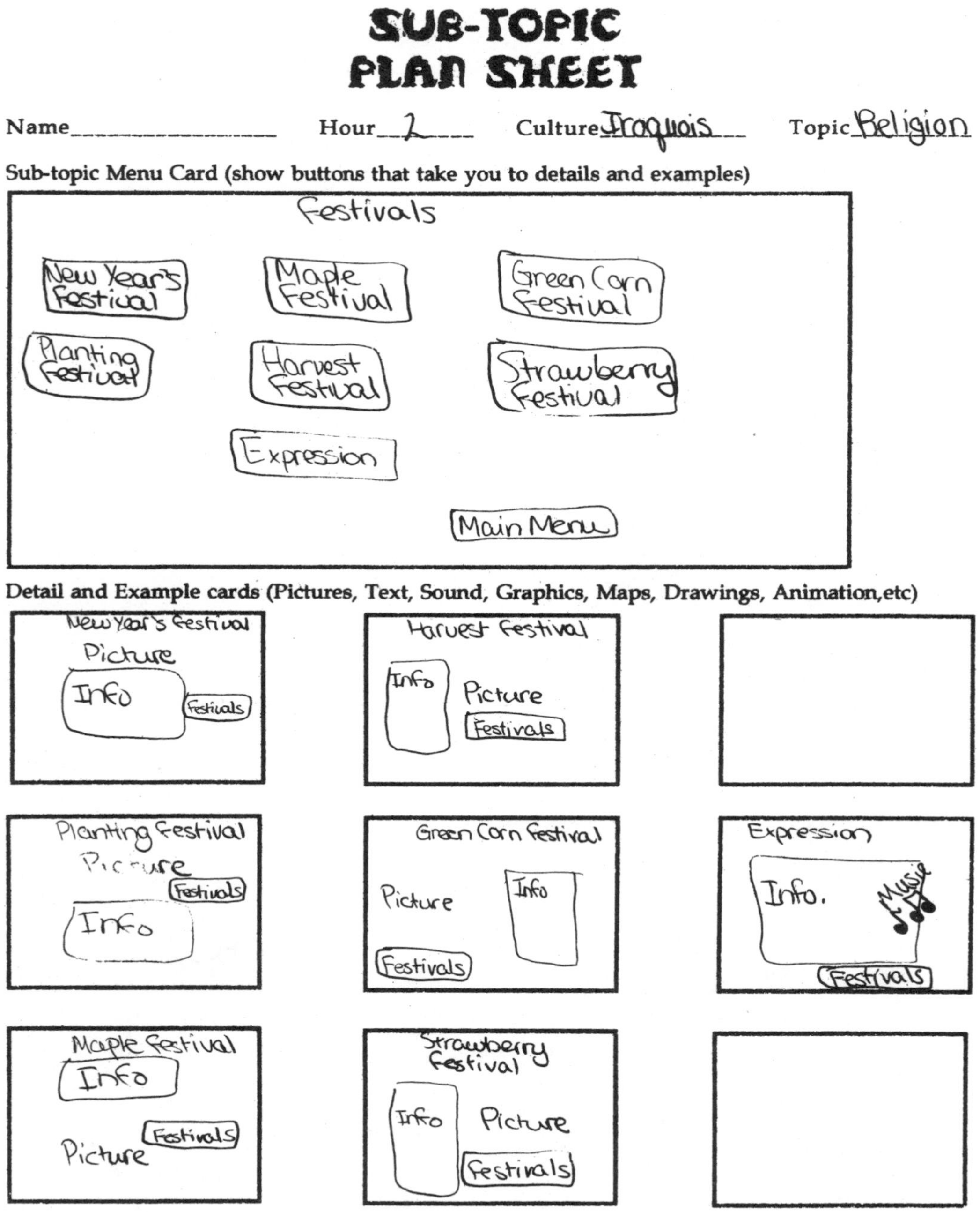

SUB-TOPIC
PLAN SHEET

Name_____ Hour__2____ Culture_Iroquois___ Topic_Religion_____

Sub-topic Menu Card (show buttons that take you to details and examples)

Festivals

New Year's Festival   Maple Festival   Green Corn Festival

Planting Festival   Harvest Festival   Strawberry Festival

Expression

Main Menu

Detail and Example cards (Pictures, Text, Sound, Graphics, Maps, Drawings, Animation, etc)

New Year's Festival
Picture
Info   Festivals

Harvest Festival
Info   Picture
Festivals

Planting Festival
Picture   Festivals
Info

Green Corn Festival
Picture   Info
Festivals

Expression
Info.   Music
Festivals

Maple Festival
Info
Picture   Festivals

Strawberry Festival
Info   Picture
Festivals

FIGURE 7.3   A subtopic plan sheet completed by a student.

to my cards so that I will remember what to do later." I shared this story with Jeff during one of our many quick hallway project conferences between classes.

I noticed my colleague's head nodding and his face wearing the same satisfied smile I wore earlier as he listened to me tell the story. He said that he had witnessed similar experiences with students in his classes. We believed that students were reflecting on their content and engaged now in how to communicate that content through plans for individual screen designs.

Each day the students made more progress on their separate subtopic plan sheets. We stressed to them that they were still in the planning phase. Right now, they were making the skeleton of their stack. Still ahead lay the task of putting the meat on those bones and giving their hypermedia document real substance. Some students found that there were veins of inquiry they had not pursued or that there were vital pieces missing from their puzzle. These students were helped in reading class to fill in those gaps. (For more on the recursive nature of the hypermedia design process, see Lehrer 1993.)

The better the skeleton was built, the sturdier their stack would be. To evaluate how well students had done, we had the students meet with their groups in a roundtable and explain their stack plan and subtopic plan sheets to the group.

During their group's discussion, Jenny asked Denise why the titles of her cards seemed to be different from the subtopic headings on her issue tree. Denise replied that she felt the titles on the cards better represented what each area of her stack was about. Satisfied with this answer, Jenny stated that she noticed that Denise had included information on famous portraits of Napoleon in her stack on art in France.

Jenny then shared that she had devoted a section of her stack of French history to Napoleon. The girls made notes on their stack plans to make an associative rather than categorical link to each other's stack. The entire group then looked for other ways they could meaningfully connect individual hyperstacks to each other and unite the separate pieces into one meaningful and coherent stack on their broad cultural question.

The group dynamic provided students the opportunity to share their strengths. Each of them was acquiring the best attributes of the group's members, because each student helped the group to evaluate and provide feedback for revisions. We believe that students' sharing their thinking processes and critical analyses gives rise to a "designing community" (Erickson 1997) with a common consciousness of process (how to do it) and standards (what criteria make a "good" one) (Erickson and Lehrer, in press).

Critical Standards and Scoring Guides: Creating an Assessment Tool

We were confident that our students had a sense of how the hypermedia software worked and a rough sense of what their hypermedia document would look like. Before they proceeded with its creation, we wanted them to know what criteria would be used to judge and assess their product. It was time to create the assessment scoring guide for our project.

It is extremely important to involve the students in the process of developing a scoring guide. We have found that students have more ownership in the criteria used to assess them if they have a hand in their creation. Teachers get a much better product, and students get what they feel is a fair and just grade. Additionally, students need practice creating and applying critical standards in all walks of life, from discerning political arguments, to buying a car and grocery shopping, to creating and reading various kinds of texts like hypermedia.

I start with a large, empty blackboard or transparency on an overhead projector. I inform the students that today they are going to be building the instrument that we will use to evaluate their projects. It is important too that students have seen some final model documents from previous years' students. (During the first year we used hypermedia documents from other sources.) Before they create this scoring guide, students need to be familiar with examples of several documents to help them think hard about what makes a good one and what to shoot for in their own stacks.

We usually start off in reading class by having students flip through three to five projects completed by previous groups of students. This gives them a sense of where they will be going and what they need to achieve. It also puts them in the role of audience, and they are reminded that their own stacks will be viewed by "dumb readers"—people who may know nothing about their topic or about hypermedia.

We would then pick out three good hyperstacks that displayed some distinct differences in terms of card quality, links, and the like. We asked the students to rank the three projects from most to least effective and then to reflect on the exact qualities that made one better than another.

During the first year of the project, when we didn't have student examples to rate, we asked students to rank hypermedia samples from their favorite software programs.

At this point, we asked the students to brainstorm what they thought needed to be part of a hypermedia document to make it successful. I listed these qualities as they offered them. Next, I asked students what things might make a hypermedia document less successful. I listed these qualities in a separate column. Since the purpose of a hypermedia document is to teach the audience something, I asked students to list the qualities of good teaching and a good teacher. What exactly is it that makes for a good learning experience when viewing hypermedia? I listed these items in a third column (see Figure 7.4).

When our brainstorming was finished, I asked students to look at the lists and try to spot common themes or repeated qualities. After they had thought about the lists for a while, I told them that we needed to classify

FIGURE 7.4   A student-generated brainstorm session on scoring guide criteria.

Brainstorm Activity to Begin Scoring Guide Construction		
Parts needed to make a hypermedia document successful	**Things that make a hypermedia document less successful**	**Qualities of good teaching and good teachers**
Organization	Only words	Humor!
Pictures	Confusing to go through	Always in a good mood
Sound	Pictures or sounds that don't fit	Likes kids
Don't get lost in stack	Boring	Excited about what they teach
Good information	Bad information or not enough	Do lots of different activities
Good spelling	Many spelling errors	Fair
Fun!	Bad grammar	Help students when they don't understand
Special effects	Buttons that don't work	Lets us work in groups
Good grammar		Listens to what we have to say
Neat buttons		More projects and less tests
Feels like a game		Time to do work in class
Keeps your attention		
Looks neat		

the list into five or six critical areas that together would pretty much ensure a good hypermedia product. Again, students were asked to perceive patterns and chunk data together. (It continually amazes us how essential design skills such as analyzing patterns, categorizing and organizing information, a sense of audience, collaborating, and revising come up again and again in terms of both our projects and real life.)

The boiled-down list that I got from each class was remarkably similar. I usually consider this a sign that there are certain observable critical areas that designate a quality product. (Wigginton 1986, and others have noted that students from across times and circumstances share very similar notions about quality teaching and learning experiences.)

There was great agreement among the students that a hypermedia document should contain a usable main menu or table of contents card (see Figure 7.5) and be connected or linked properly so that the browser or audience would not get lost. (You can obtain the whole stack, as well as other examples of student stacks, at our book web site.) Navigation is

FIGURE 7.5   Printout of a main menu or table of contents card.

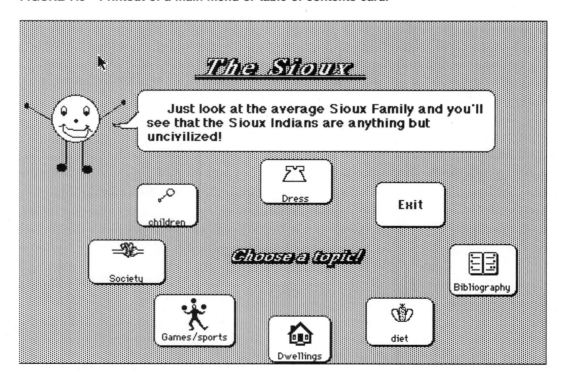

key. Classes agreed that each document must include good information. "Good" was eventually discussed in terms of information that is correct, relevant, important, thorough, accountable, and accessible. The information would answer the research question, could be verified through various sources, and could be understood by a novice. There was also a consensus that spelling and correct language usage were important. (Remember that this is how students were articulating their own criteria.)

Most classes included audience involvement in their criteria, a quality they drew from their list of what makes good teaching. They told me that if the audience was involved, then they weren't bored or tuned out, so there was more of a chance that they would be learning. In one class Jenny explained, "When a book is interesting, I want to keep reading it and I remember it better."

Roberto agreed: "I always pay more attention to TV shows and movies that make me feel like I'm there . . . like I'm in the movie or something."

I always attempted to make students clarify what they meant by audience involvement in terms of this electronic media by asking them to give me examples of good audience involvement. In one class, Sheila pointed out to me that we "sort of need to entertain our audience."

I asked Sheila if she thought it was possible for us to entertain and teach at the same time. Melissa came to Sheila's rescue and pointed out that we had listed humor as a key element in good teaching—"Like you. You always make me laugh, and sometimes you teach me something that I didn't know," Melissa joked.

I shared a laugh with the class at the reference to "learning sometimes." I thanked Melissa for her backhanded compliment to my teaching efficiency. "You're welcome!" she replied, smiling slyly.

During this time, Sheila provided me with her own example of entertaining education: "My little brother has a CD program that he plays all the time. The program teaches him math and reading, but he thinks he is playing games with a lion cub. The lion cub acts like a guide that takes him through the program. One of the stacks we saw in reading class had something like that [see Figure 7.6]. The author had included a little circle character that took us through her stack. I kept looking for that little guy as we went through the stack. The little guy made the stack more interesting so I paid closer attention. I actually remember some of the stuff that little guy said!"

I responded, "I agree that the little guy was a great way to involve the audience. Can anyone think of other ways we could involve them?" The class quickly came up with things like interactive quizzes (see Figure 7.7),

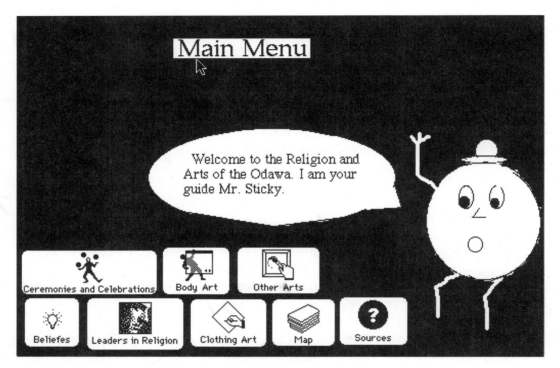

FIGURE 7.6   Printout showing the use of a guide for a stack.

as well as game show themes, questions throughout the text, animations, special effects, and sound. Some of these attributes they had seen in stacks we had shown them, and others they drew from software programs that they liked.

The last area that was usually identified was the inclusion of different media, like pictures and sound. I had to push my classes the hardest to get this quality out of them. Although these kids were growing up in a multimedia world, they seemed to be stuck to the written word when it came to their own creative design process. This too is going to change as the tools of technology become more accessible. We pushed our groups hard to make their documents truly interactive and multimedia.

The next day I showed all the classes what had been produced in each of the other classes. Students enjoyed comparing and contrasting the criteria that had been included. Most were amazed to see how much agreement there was on the criteria chosen. Jenny raised her hand, and I called on her: "Wow, that is way cool. We all think the same way."

So you want to leave, do 'ya? You know, people don't normally make it out of here alive... C'mon, make my day! (I can't remember which one I'm supposed to say. It's on of the two. They're suppose to scare you.) But since I hate to see such interesting people so scared, I _____guess I can make a deal. I'll give you the secret on getting out of here alive if you can answer my three questions. (I need to them for a quiz at my school.) Okay., deal? All right, here they are.

```
#1:  Give  one  name  of  a  game  played
by  the  Sioux.
```

Main Menu

La Crosse

Trinket

Basketball

FIGURE 7.7   Card printout of a quiz example.

I followed Jenny's comment with a question: "Are you sure you think the same way?"

Jenny answered, "Sure. Just look at the qualities from each class. They're practically the same."

I looked at the whole class as I responded, "Jenny is right. The areas chosen are pretty much the same. What we have to do today is determine what we really mean by each criterion."

Jenny questioned back, "What do you mean?"

I told the class that without specific description, their criteria were very vague. "For instance, each class included a criterion that states that a good hypermedia document contained good information, right?"

The class nodded its agreement. We were at a crucial point now where evaluative criteria are translated into *benchmarks,* or specific descriptions of what the criteria will look like when fully manifested. In other words, what exact features will help us recognize the achievement of a particular criterion? (See the worksheet in Figure 7.8.)

"But what do you mean by *good?*" I asked them. "Does *good* information mean that there is a lot of information or that it is well written?"

The class stopped nodding and started thinking. Denise volunteered

---

Model Questioning Sequence: Assessing Our Product

What is one feature that needs to be included in an excellent product?
Good information

What are the qualities that show information is excellent?
Is correct
Answers research question
Is thorough, interesting, engaging to audience
Is specific

How do we know the information is correct?
Comes from credible sources
Comes from multiple sources
Can be verified

How do we know the information answers the research question?

FIGURE 7.8　Worksheet to help connect and come up with features that help us recognize the achievement of a particular criterion.

her thoughts, "I think it means both. I mean you should have a lot of information, and it should be written well also."

I asked another question to deepen their quandary. "That's good, Denise, but how much is *a lot* of information? What do you mean by that?"

Now the class was shaking its collective head. I eased their frustration by explaining that those were the decisions we had to make today. Clearly, without a specific description, or benchmark, our criteria could mean many things to many people. The class nodded its agreement again. I told them that I wanted them to understand clearly what they had to do to get the best grade possible.

Since they were seventh graders, they should know best what good seventh-grade work should look like. That was one of the reasons why I was including them in building the evaluation instrument.

Jenny raised her hand, "I think we should add this to our list of qualities of good teaching."

I said, "I think we just did."

We continued to work on a good description for our criterion on information. I directed the discussion by having students first work on a description of what information would look like in the best or a very high-quality hypermedia document. Once we had established that, I explained that we would also have to describe what other levels of quality or proficiency would look like. Unfortunately, not everyone would fit the high-quality description.

Jenny asked, "How many descriptions do we need then?"

I could sense her worry that we would have to create descriptions until she had nightmares about them. I relieved their fears by saying, "I think three levels of proficiency should be enough. We will make ones for Distinguished, Competent, and Not Yet Competent." Once I explained what Competent meant, we continued. Students found it relatively easy to construct descriptions for Competent and Not Yet Competent once Distinguished was done.

We worked our way through the criteria. The toughest one to describe proved to be the criterion for including different media. We were stuck. Neither my classes nor I could come up with a way to describe even a distinguished level of proficiency that everyone could agree on. We thought that requiring a picture or sound on every screen or card was too much because, as someone pointed out, sometimes a certain amount of blank space is good. We couldn't put a number on how many pictures or sounds must be included because each stack was unique and different in its scheme and scope. I was ending most classes with a big question mark covering the spot where the description should be.

During just such a struggle in one class, a usually quiet and shy girl raised her hand. "Yes, Nicole?" I asked, giving her the floor.

"What if the author could justify that she had thoughtfully used the space of each screen?"

The room became very quiet. I stood there staring dumbfounded at Nicole, who was turning red believing she had said something wrong or that might be perceived as dumb. I finally spoke, rescuing her. "That is brilliant, Nicole! It's simple and suits our purposes for this project perfectly." The class applauded spontaneously—I think as much for relief of their frustration as for Nicole's stroke of brilliance. In the end, the appearance is more important, and it appeared that the class was applauding Nicole. I joined them. Now Nicole's blush was joined by a big smile, one made all the bigger by the smallness of its owner.

Nicole's class reminded me of another good reason for including students in the process of developing the scoring guide. Many times the students came up with better ideas than I did. We felt that this is what it

SCORING GUIDE FOR HYPER PROJECT ASSESSMENT

Disk Number_____   Hour_____   Topic_____   Number of Cards_____   TOTAL POINTS _____

Critiqued by #_____

CRITERIA	DISTINGUISHED			COMPETENT			NOT-YET-COMPETENT			COMMENTS
Multimedia Card Space Justification PTS____	12 OR 10 PTS 1 bad cd per 10 cds 2 max.			8 PTS 2 bad cds per 10 4 max.			4 PTS 3+ bad cds per 10 5+ total			
	Card space has been thoughtfully used and use of multimedia sources has been considered throughout the stack. Author can justify space use if asked.									1 2 3 4 5 6 7 8 9 10
Stack Organization and function PTS____	12 17+ cds 2 probs.	OR 12-16 cds 1 prob.	10 PTS 11 or less 0 problems	8 PTS 17+ cds 3 probs.	12-16 2 probs.	11 or less 1 problem	17+ cds 4+ probs.	12-16 cds 3+ probs.	4 PTS 11 or less 2+ probs.	
	Stack organization follows an easy to use Main Menu or Table of Contents card. Organization allows the audience to go through the stack in a way that is informative and makes sense.									1 2 3 4 5 6 7 8 9 10
Information Quality PTS____	12 11 10 9 Text is **interesting** to read and written in the author's own words **throughout** the stack. There are **no gaps** in the coverage of the topic or C.F.			8 7 6 5 **Most** of stack is **interesting** to read and written in author's own words. Coverage of the topic and C.F. is **adequate** but could be better.			4 PTS **Most** of stack is **not** interesting to read. Much of the text seems to be copied. Topic/C.F. is **not covered**.			
Spelling and Grammar Quality PTS____	12 11 10 9 0 1-2 3-4 5 Total errors not more than 1 per cd or maximum of ..... total in stack.			8 7 6 6 7 8 Total errors not more than 2 per cd or a maximum of ..... total in stack			4 PTS **9+ ERRORS** More than 9 errors.			(Spelling, Capitalization, Punctuation) 1 2 3 4 5 6 7 8 9 10
Research Quality PTS____	12 11+ Stack contains a bibliography card with different types of sources written in the required format. Points assigned according to **Total sources** as shown above.	10 9-10		8 5-8			4 PTS <5			(Books, Encyclopedia, Magazines, Internet, Pamphlet, Interview, CD-ROM, Video) Total Sources = 1 2 3 4 5 6 7 8 9 10
Button Quality PTS____	12 1 PROBLEM PER 5 CDS Reasons for all links and button names are clear and warranted. Author has used icons and effects that help the audience understand stack organization and content.	OR	10	8 1 PROBLEM PER 3 CDS			2+ PROBS PER 3 CDS		4 PTS	1 2 3 4 5 6 7 8 9 10
Audience Consideration PTS____	12 5+ attempts A variety of attempts have been made throughout the stack to involve the audience in an interesting and engaging way. The stack feels like interactive software.	10 4 attempts		8 3 attempts to involve audience			< 3 attempts		4 PTS	(Pictures 3=1, Animation, Format Graphic, Quiz, Use Questions, Authentic Sound, Game, Video, Scripted Effects)

FIGURE 7.9   Student-created scoring guide in its final form.

meant to become a "facilitator of learning" rather than a "keeper of the knowledge." We have to believe facilitation is better. After all, my students were very involved in their learning process and that was on their list of qualities of good teaching.

As the classes worked through this process, I helped expedite it. I suggested uniform criterion labels and categories so that each class worked toward the same goal. I also used my expertise and experience to suggest categories and descriptors. I was careful not to take ownership away from the students. I wanted them to feel and know that they created the instrument that would hold them accountable and ultimately determine their grade. When the criteria areas and proficiency descriptors were complete, I suggested using a Likert scale for assigning points across the levels of proficiency. I explained to the students how it worked and they were accepting of it.

I pointed out that there was always going to be some measure of subjectivity to the evaluation process but that we had a tool (see Figure 7.9) that should help us be as fair as possible. (In Chapter 8 we explain how the student-design scoring tool was used for reflection, peer critiquing, and peer assessment.)

Preparing for the Computer Lab

Now we were ready to help students move on to providing more detailed planning. I proudly hauled out the card planning and justification sheets with a smile. (Jeff often kidded me about liking the form enough to marry it. I reflected on this and replied that there were times that I was spending more time perfecting the card plan sheet than I was spending with my wife.)

Exploring relatively uncharted teaching territory was not only time-consuming but tough to stay on top of and manage. A project with computers was especially difficult in our school because there was only one computer lab. We had to get the most out of the time reserved in the lab because there was always someone else waiting to get classes in. Another problem was that we worked primarily with old Macintosh LCs or Mac Classics. When a few PowerMacs arrived, there was great competition to get on those machines.

The card plan/justification sheet was the tool that made computer lab time most meaningful and productive. We had come up with two forms of individual card planning sheets to meet the needs of our students. These card plan sheets were the next step in the stack planning sequence. Students were asked to use the forms to make detailed plans for each card they had roughed out on their stack plan sheet.

One sheet (Figure 7.10) resembled a storyboard format. Kirsten favored this form because it allowed her to think about her card in three different parts, which helped her focus during the designing process. She used the first box to create a general likeness of her card. The second box she used for her text or information about sound and video clips. Kirsten liked the last box best, because it allowed her to write notes to herself (and a justification to her peers and teachers for what she was doing) about how a button would look; why, when clicked with the mouse, it would move the browser to the card it did; and why a specific special transition effect was attached to this movement.

Jenny preferred the second form, which looked more like the final

HYPERMEDIA PLANNING SHEET

Title of Project_____   Name Kirsten_____   Hr. 2

Directions: Use this sheet to plan the screens of your stack. You may want to label the screen to help you keep track of your organization.

Screen Layout	Text/Audio	Notes
Screen # **Iroquois Meeting PROCEDURES** See Text/Audio Wampum MR Emain Menu	whenever ∧ The Iroquois called a meeting it would usually last from 2-3 days. It was a large gathering of tribes from all over the state. Everyone who had something to say, (which was usually most everyone) was expected to say it, which helps acount for the long time span of the meeting. For you to speak, you must be holding the Hiawatha wampum belt. This symbolizes peace and the founding of the Confederacy. the ∧ A number of days before a meeting would be spread by decorated messengers. They would carry an stick with them. The number of notches on the stick showed	wampum belt goes to animation of speaking procedure. very long!

Screen # The Wampum Belt
 	
 See Text/ Audio
 	
 MR Animation Picture Back
	how many days till the meeting.
	 ~~Silence while others were talking~~ was expected.
	  The only way you could speak during a meeting was if you were holding the Hiawatha Wampum Belt. This belt symbolized peace and the founding of the Iroquois Confederacy.
	  The pattern has a figure almost like a tree in the center with squares coming off it.
	  The belt is made of wampum beads. They were brought over by they Europeans through the fur trade.
		links to?

FIGURE 7.10   A storyboard sheet completed by a student.

HYPERMEDIA PLANNING SHEET

Title of Project_____   Name Kirsten_____ Hr. 2

Directions: Use this sheet to plan the screens of your stack. You may want to label the screen to help you keep track of your organization.

Screen Layout	Text/Audio	Notes
Screen # 1 — The Government of the Iroquois Indians. See Text/Audio. (boxes labeled: leaders, procedure, Clans, bibliography, rules)	The central focus of this stack is how the government of the Iroquois Indians helped to shape the U.S. government system. Each subtopic card will outline an important aspect to government. Animation and interactive questions will help to further explain my points. I hope you find my stack interesting and helpful. Enjoy!	goes to subtopic
Screen # — Iroquois Clans. See Text/Audio. (boxes labeled: leaders, To MM)	Clans were the main life system of Iroquois society. Each had their own name and symbol. Bear, fox, and wolf are some examples. To be a leader of the clan, you had to be well respected, a powerful speaker, or brave.	quiz here

FIGURE 7.10   continued

product on her computer screen (see Figure 7.11). She could closely depict the card as it would actually look, as well as write her text as it would appear on the screen.

Jenny favored the organized notes and justification section located at the bottom of this form. She felt it prompted her to make design notes and to explain why she was doing what she was. It was this metacognitive part of both sheets that we liked most. We felt that it not only made students explain their thinking and be critical of their product but also forced students to consider their audience. At the same time, we constantly reminded students to consider the criteria on the scoring guide

FIGURE 7.11   A card plan/justification sheet completed by a student.

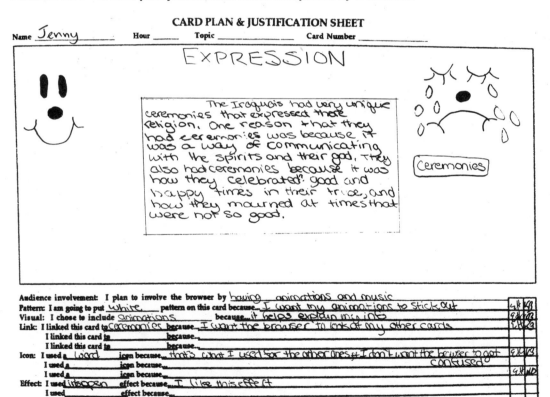

while designing their cards (i.e., what aspects make a hypermedia document "good" and what to shoot for).

We agreed that the card plan sheets made students more productive in the computer lab. I remembered a previous student, Anna, who had at first labeled the forms unneeded "busywork." Later in the project, Anna had become not only a believer but a vocal advocate of the use of the card plan forms. Anna had come up to me in the computer lab and quietly admitted that the forms really seemed to help her get a lot done. "I don't have to take time inventing what I am going to do next, because I already did that when I made the sheets." Then Anna asked, "But will I get downgraded if some things I do don't match the sheets?"

I asked her what she meant.

Anna said, "Well, it's just that sometimes I see a better way to do something while I'm sitting at the computer."

I assured her that this was fine and pointed out that she never could have made that kind of critical revision if she had not done the card plan sheet first. Anna rolled her eyes and said, "Man, you really love those sheets, don't you?"

I confided to Anna that I had put a lot of thought, effort, and myself into the design forms. I was proud of them in the same way she was proud of her completed hypermedia project.

Jenny was again holding some papers in my face. This time she held her five completed card plans and asked me if this was enough to earn her admittance to the computer lab. I took the plans and looked to see that the text had been initialed by Pat, the language arts teacher. Jenny's plans had all been initialed by Pat and other student critics for grammar and content. I knew that Pat had spent considerable time working with the students on developing a topic and writing from research notes, so I asked Jenny how she felt about the writing part of doing the card plans.

Jenny responded that the writing was still not easy, but it was clear what she was supposed to do. I agreed that writing was not easy but then reminded her that few things worth doing are easy to do. This was little comfort to Jenny, but she sighed and nodded her head nonetheless.

I then made Jenny's day by saying, "Yes, now you have your ticket but before . . ." I was interrupted by an exasperated Jenny.

"Ugh, why does there always have to be a before?!?!?"

I laughed at her dramatic transescent (adolescent in transition) display. "First," I said, "I'm going to show you some special effects that you can put in your stack."

Jenny relaxed and said, "Well, that's different."

I liked to show the students some of the more advanced possibilities that the software provided them. I call these effects and possibilities "advanced," but anyone can master them with the help of a good reference book on the software (such as *The Complete HyperCard 2.2 Handbook* or *HyperCard 2.2 in a Hurry*). I demonstrated that computer text can be more than just text. It can also be a doorway or a hotlink connection to further information or related ideas.

The effect of a hotlink or hot text is one that most of my students have experienced on the World Wide Web. I like to point out this similarity and explain to my students that the concept of hot text came from the software they are using and what they are learning has direct applications on the World Wide Web. I also like to get the classes excited over animation sequences and other special effects, since I am more the "techie" part of our teaching team. I reminded them that we all learn best at different speeds and in different ways, and this tool would allow them to apply what they had learned.

I closed with a note of caution. The special effects and drawing tools that were available to students were a lot of fun and integral to making an excellent hypermedia document—but they could also be a pitfall. Making use of these tools was time-consuming, and in some cases students could get off on a tangent and lose track of their goal. That is why we constantly stressed that students must know how everything served the purposes of their document. Through guided discussion, students remembered that their larger purpose was to create a high-quality hypermedia document. Computer lab time was at a premium, so students needed to take responsibility for managing their time (Lehrer 1993).

Moving to the Computers

We could not hold our students back any longer. Computer lab time had arrived. The students who had completed previous phases of the project excitedly entered the computer lab to begin what they considered the "fun" work. Those who were not yet prepared for lab time became exceptionally motivated to do what was necessary to join their classmates on the computers.

We had reserved lab time in relation to the research time the students had put in. We knew from experience that creating a hypermedia document from solid, thorough research could take three to five weeks at the seventh-grade level. We were convinced that the educational gains made this time well spent. Again, we were spending a lot of time on the project, but we believe that less is more, especially if students can learn foundational competencies through long-term engagement with a project.

As students entered the computer lab, they were required to show me at least five card plans completed and initialed by teachers and peers. I generally let students sit near people they are comfortable with. Only minor adjustments usually had to be made to ensure that the computer lab environment would be conducive to work rather than socialization. I got everyone started on the right foot by leading the class through the steps of correctly naming and starting a new hypermedia document. I reminded students that they must be productive and said, for the hundredth time, "Don't waste your lab time!"

Jenny moaned and replied, "I've been working so hard to get in here. Do you really think I'm going to waste time now that I'm here?"

No response was necessary on my part. If Jenny and her classmates felt that way, then Jeff and I had been successful in giving our students the feeling that they had earned this opportunity. Chances are they would not take it lightly.

While I was in the computer lab with some students, Jeff had other students in his room still working on card plans or revisions from student or teacher critiques. Our homework assignments during the computer lab time required students to complete two more card plans per day. The new card plans would then be checked, critiqued, and revised during the class of the teacher who was not in the computer lab that day. As part of the integration of our teaching, we would switch off assisting in the classroom versus the computer lab.

Students who could not produce the card plans at the door of the lab were sent to the critiquing and revising classroom to finish. Students were thus held accountable. We often used this "work stations" technique to best serve the needs of the students (Erickson 1997). The blocking of time in this manner created larger sustained work periods, productive for both the students and teachers. We both found it refreshing to change our focus occasionally by switching from the classroom to computer lab. The change maintained our energy level and interest through the project.

We both knew that regardless of who was in the computer lab, that person would have to wear running shoes and a problem-solving cap. If we had twenty-three students in a class sitting at twenty-three computers, there was potential for twenty-three completely different problems. (We said that we always felt that we were earning our pay when we were working in the lab. Although it was tiring, it was a good tired. We felt a rewarding tired that reminded us that we were making a difference.)

The kids were working equally hard. If someone wanted to know how to do a newly discovered special effect, I would yell out for help from any other student who had done the new special effect. Someone who had used that special effect would go to the student who needed help to peer-tutor the person. Sometimes kids suggested students from other classes or a previous year's class who could be solicited to staff the lab and help solve problems. At other times, kids had to find out something on their own by reading a manual or through trial and error. In this way, expertise, particularly about design features, did not reside within the teacher; rather, it was developed by and resided as distributed expertise throughout the school community (Brown et al. 1993; Erickson 1997; Lehrer et al. 1994).

We kept several software reference books on hand so that challenges could be solved as they arose. Along with this preventive planning, we took several other measures to make the computer lab experience as positive and productive as possible. First, all students were taught a routine of always backing up and saving their project in more than one location. For us, this was on a floppy disk and on the hard drive of the computer each student sat at each day.

Next, we created help sheets for the HyperMedia design software, scanner, and other hardware devices and software programs that we used. The help sheets listed all the steps, from beginning to end, for successful use of a hardware device or software program. For the HyperMedia software program, the help sheets provided instructions for using the basic tools of the program to create a hypermedia document. Eventually we would provide students with help sheets that would provide hints, reminders, and shortcuts for adding animations, sound, pictures, and more advanced programming techniques. (You can obtain copies of our help sheets at our book web site.)

We taped help sheets next to each computer, the scanner, and other hardware devices and encouraged students to use them. We encouraged students to seek peer help by adhering to an "Ask three students before you ask me" philosophy. Students found that most of their problems and questions could be answered by their classmates. We also kept a supply of floppy disks on hand to replace the ones that inevitably failed. Finally, Jeff and I made sure that all students locked up or protected their document with provisions of the software.

The biggest challenge we encountered came not from the computers or the software but from the students. The challenge, however, was a positive one. I remember the day that one of the teachers in our team came rushing up to me to ask me what special effects and advanced techniques I had shown the students. After hearing a recap of my special effects presentation, my colleague got a distant look on her face. I asked what was wrong as she took a step back. She asked how, if that was what I had shown the students, Tony had just shown her a completely different special effect he had added to his hypermedia document.

I responded, "After only one week! You must be kidding!"

I could tell that she was very serious and ran to the lab to see for myself. It was true. Tony had mastered a completely new special effect that I had not taught. He had apparently spent all of his study hall time plus after school working on this special effect with one of the software reference books at his side. I ran back upstairs to my colleague and said, "Man, this is dangerous! The students have more time than we do, and their knowledge of the power of this software program is likely to grow exponentially."

She could only say, "I know."

The whole team then brainstormed how we could harness and direct this newfound powerful knowledge. News of the new special effect and the untold other possibilities was likely to spread faster than word of the latest breakup of a teenage romance. It was important to keep this newly empowered group of students on the White side of the Force (the good side in the Star Wars movies). We knew these students could just as easily look for ways to be mischievous with this newfound power.

The next day we decided that some of these advanced students should help their classmates with their daily challenges whenever possible. Tony was especially receptive to this suggestion. Tony had previously struggled in the classroom and now found himself in the new role of the "smart" kid as peer tutor, a role he cherished. This type of reversal of roles was common in all the classes we taught. We agreed that this showed the power of the computer as a tool and design as an instructional process. Once again, we were seeing students at all levels being challenged and empowered to design their own learning at the same time. This thought always made that tired feeling we shared from a week of intensive student interaction a rewarding one.

A Cautionary Tale: Beware of Trash with Flash

Tony continued to push the medium of hypermedia, but not always with the requisite attention to what he was trying to communicate to an audience with his document. When he had mastered one special effect, he went on to experiment with another more sophisticated one. He created an animation for his Transportation in Norway stack that featured a school bus crashing through a speed limit sign and a highway barrier before diving down a cliff to a fiery end in a Norwegian fjord. Tony was the toast of the town until we asked him what this demonstrated about traveling in Norway. Did Norway have dangerous roads? Were speed limits posted in miles per hours? Were there many school bus accidents in Norway? Should people traveling to Scandinavia avoid buses?

Tony was sent packing to the library, where he found that Norway has the safest road system in Europe and no recorded school bus accidents. He also learned about European highway signs and that most of the world uses kilometers per hours on their speed limit signs.

A day later, Tony called me over to his computer. "I fixed it!" Tony exulted. He had added an introductory card that said, "To see something that would never happen in Norway, push this button." His beloved animation followed, along with an explanation of the safe nature of Norwegian roads.

We all had a good laugh, but the story demonstrates the power of computer flash and the vigilance that must be used to keep this flash working for the White side of the Force.

Chapter 8

Getting It Right

Important Points

This chapter explains how students are taught to reflect on and revise their hypermedia documents and illustrates the critiquing process at the card and stack level. It discusses the creation of a design community of students with a common set of critical standards and concludes with ideas and methods for assessing hypermedia projects.

➡ It is important to have multiple levels of evaluation with any significant task. Students need to be assessed by experts such as teachers, by peers, and by themselves.

➡ Assessment requires a shared understanding of criteria, or qualities and clear descriptions of what makes a piece of work "good."

➡ Students can be taught how to peer-critique and evaluate their own and each others' hypermedia stacks based on these shared criteria.

➡ Students need to understand that completing a product does not mean they are done. They are not done until all criteria are met and all audiences satisfied. Using assessment feedback to make revisions is a critical step in completing a satisfactory project.

➡ Revision can mean correcting surface-level problems like spelling and grammar, but it also means deeply "re-seeing" and restructuring the document as a whole to fit more closely to the author's purposes to communicate important meanings.

I know what revision means now. It means finding all kinds of reasons from all kinds of people about why what you thought was pretty hot really needs to be re-thought, re-looked at, and redone about seventeen more times!

Sean, seventh grader

If you do not have a clear sense of the key dimensions of a sound performance—a vision of poor and outstanding performance—you can neither teach students to perform nor evaluate their performance.

R. Stiggins (1987)

Of course it's hard, but it's the hard that makes it good!

Tom Hanks, in the film *A League of Their Own*

Continuous reflection, assessment, and revision had been structured into the project from the start. In fact, although we have discussed the different elements of the design process one at a time as distinct phases, much of what we did was recursive (Lehrer et al. 1994). Students reframed questions throughout the process, continually saw the need to find more find information, consistently reviewed and revised what they were working on. Informal teacher-, peer-, and self-assessment of process and product occurred daily as we continuously improved and rethought our ongoing projects.

Our purpose was to bring students to the point where they would self-evaluate their performance on all phases of the research and design process. At this point, they would internalize a variety of tools and strategies for self-critique. We wanted them to learn to value and solicit the advice of others, and know how to give advice to others. We wanted them to recognize, apply, and continually coach themselves and each other in the development of critical standards in each skill area of design (Erickson and Lehrer, in press).

We conducted short roundtables to critique individual cards early in the design phase, and then later had students present their complete stacks to groups of peer critics. It was an especially compelling testimony to the power of real audiences and peer critique that most organizational revisions and the inclusion of most links to related information occurred after peer revision of entire stacks (Lehrer et al. 1993, 1994). We have found that it is often easier to evaluate another person's work than it is our own.

In Chapter 7, we discussed continuous kinds of assessment that were daily and weekly spot checks and reorientations of our process of learning and design. In this chapter, we discuss more focused kinds of informal assessments of actual products and then the formal assessment of the final product of a stack of cards.

Quality Counts!

As students progressed through the process of designing and concluding their stacks in the computer lab, it was time to think about ensuring that their actual computer-generated product was of a high quality and met the students' own articulated critical standards for quality.

We have found that it is best if most students have completed or nearly completed their stacks before they make formal presentations to peers and ask for a final round of holistic feedback. We usually allow about three weeks in the lab before expecting completed hypermedia documents. When most students have finished, it's time for the fine-tuning. We start this process with peer critiquing.

Card-Level Critique

Students must be taught how to critique. This kind of teaching is worth repeating, and so we emphasized and reemphasized how to work together critically and productively throughout the year.

We did card-level critique, for example, at a variety of points during the design phase. We would display a newly minted student card and might spend a few minutes at the beginning of class critiquing it. This focused the students' attention wonderfully.

At the beginning of one class during the design phase, Monica volunteered to share a card that she had just created (see Figure 8.1). I (Jeff) reminded the students to use the P-Q-P (praise-question-polish) model of peer critique. On this day, I used Monica's card to model a peer critique. Then pairs of students were to share their hypermedia cards and critique the screen designs.

"What should we be seeing, feeling, and hearing both now and when

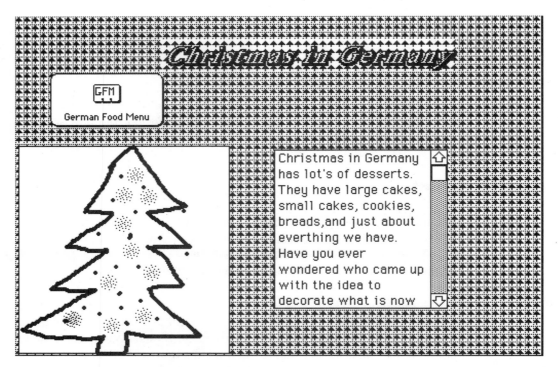

FIGURE 8.1   Card printout of Monica's Christmas in Germany card.

we work in pairs later?" I asked the group. They responded with comments like, "People should be listening to each other and nodding." "The designer should feel good about what they've done, but should know what to do to make it even better!" "We should be asking questions instead of judging stuff."

I then asked, "What should I *not* be seeing, hearing, or feeling?" In this way, they were reminded that feedback should be given in an appropriate and supportive way.

I displayed Monica's card on Christmas in Germany, which was part of her stack answering the question, "How are holidays important to the Germans?"

The class started by praising Monica for creating her own graphic of a Christmas tree. The information on the card fit her topic, her group's overall topic on the family culture of Germany, and her own questions of interest. The class was intrigued that the original idea of Christmas trees, or *Christbaume,* and the idea of decorating trees came from Germany. They learned from Monica's card that almost all Germans still decorate their trees with candles, which they light only on Christmas Eve or *Heilige Abend* (Holy Evening). Presents are also opened on Christmas Eve because the Germans believe that this is when Christ received his gifts.

A couple of students uttered surprise that Christmas seemed so much more religiously oriented in Germany than here in America. The students also liked Monica's button design communicating a link/connection to other cards about Recipes and Easter.

Then the questions started. Why hadn't she linked this card to her "May Day" card, which she had displayed a week earlier? Monica answered that she was only linking religious holidays to this card. Weren't there other religious holidays in Germany? Yes, the day of Prayer and Repentance (*Buss und Bet-Tag*), for example, was a holiday she had just found out about. She promised to make a link to that and to a card on St. Michael's Day. The class helped Monica to examine the relationships among her content through their feedback on links (connections) to other cards.

The class then focused attention on the text that Monica had written on this screen. What kinds of cakes and breads? Which ones were similar to ours? Which were different? There was general agreement that Monica had not been specific enough in her writing. Several students wanted to know what kinds of presents Germans gave and how many they tended to exchange and with whom.

And why hadn't she made her text field bigger instead of scrolling it? (A *field* is where the text is placed in a box on the screen. There are several options to authors as to the type of field.) They pointed out that she could use her space better by filling up the background with a bigger text field and more imagery.

Anne suggested that Monica record in a favorite German Christmas carol to supplement her information with sound. Attention then turned to Monica's graphic of a tree. Why hadn't she included the candles and cranberry strings she had written about in her text? Her graphic should reflect her text and add information consistent with the text. Several times both the students and Monica had a good laugh, especially about Monica's lack of proofreading. Nevertheless, the tone was very respectful, and it was clear that the students were having fun, the kind of "hard fun" that Papert (1996) and Negroponte (1995) say is possible with computer design.

A lot of the students' questions had included implicit suggestions for polishing. I concluded by praising Monica for her progress and the class for their highly insightful critiques.

I paired the class off and reminded the pairs, as they began to peer-critique a card from each other's stack, to consider all of the hard work everyone had done and that our purpose was to help each other, not hurt—to critique instead of criticize. This process had taken about eight minutes. Pairs worked with each other for another eight to twelve minutes. As a result, everyone still had at least twenty-five minutes to continue design work and revisions.

Stack-Level Critique

In addition to critiquing individual cards, at the end of the project students needed to critique their stacks as a whole, to ensure that all cards (screens) worked together in a coherent structure to communicate their information to their audience. I liked to start this phase of the project by reviewing the criteria and proficiency levels we had developed together as a class in our assessment scoring guide. I reminded the students of the discussions we had when we developed this scoring guide.

Although students were encouraged to use the guide throughout the project and we often referred to it, it took many students until this activity to realize the deficiencies in their stacks. This activity alone usually causes many students to see the gaps in their information or their stack and how they measure up against the criteria we set forth for good stacks (Erickson 1997; Lehrer 1993; Lehrer et al. 1994).

After reviewing the scoring guide, students needed to apply it to a stack other than their own. We modeled this procedure as a whole class. In this case, it is important for all students to see the stack that is being used as a classroom example. There are many ways to do this. One way is by using a data display to project the stack onto a screen for all to see. Another is to load the stack onto the computer lab server so that it could be opened from every computer in the lab. A low-tech way is to copy printed-out screens onto transparencies and use the overhead projector to go through them one at a time. This technique had the advantage that we could use it back in the classroom, without computers.

Since we had been working previously with Andy's information, I (Paul) asked him if we could critique his stack. He said everyone already knew everything else about his project, so it didn't matter to him. It wouldn't be necessary to use Andy's stack as an example, but it did provide familiar ground for the class. I chose to display Andy's stack on a screen in front of the class. This allowed me to control movement through the stack and clearly point things out for the students.

First, I handed out a critiquing procedure sheet to the students (see Figure 8.2). We went through the stack to get a general impression, which we discussed as a class. I took them back through each criterion on the scoring guide (see Figure 7.9). I made sure to point out to the class that I expected them to follow the same procedure when they critiqued stacks on their own. Students need to have their critiquing procedure sheet and a blank scoring guide in front of them when critiquing each stack. (See our book web site for a copy of these documents.)

Our scoring guide lists several criteria and benchmarks for different levels of proficiency. The first criterion was "multimedia card space justification." I asked the class what level of proficiency they thought Andy had reached regarding this criterion. Was he Distinguished, Competent, or Not Yet Competent?

Jenny raised her hand. "Most of the cards in his stack have the space

FIGURE 8.2   Stack critiquing procedure sheet.

Stack Critiquing Procedure Sheet

The following steps are a guide for you to follow when critiquing a stack. *Remember, all completed scoring guides must have critical notes to the author written in the appropriate areas.*

1. Skim through the stack rather quickly. Try to get an overall feel for what the author has done.
2. Spell-check the stack. To do this, open the message box (Option-m) and type in Spellcheck. This will activate hyperspeller, which you will then use to check the spelling throughout the stack. Keep track of errors on your scoring guide.
3. Now start at the beginning of the stack and go through it slowly. Be sure to read and examine each card carefully. Take your time! Write notes in the space provided on the scoring guide in each critical area when appropriate.
4. You should now be ready to score the stack for information quality.
5. Next score it for audience consideration.
6. Decide on a score for multimedia card space use.
7. Score the stack for organization.
8. Score the stack for button quality.
9. Go to the stack's bibliography card, and score the stack for research quality.

used well. But . . ." Jenny hesitated. Despite the multiple times we had done whole-class critiques, I could tell she was still reluctant to critique someone openly, so I said, "Go ahead, Jenny. We know you're only being honest and trying to help Andy have the best stack possible. It doesn't help anyone if we aren't honest in our critiques."

Clearly there are many social issues involved in this type of learning, so we worked hard to create and maintain a healthy culture of peer critique and peer assistance. It worked, but required constant vigilance.

Andy smiled at Jenny, so she continued, "But there are several cards that could be made to look better."

"In what way, Jenny?" I asked.

"Well, I'm not saying he has to have a picture on every card but . . . go to that card on 'The Background of Dance' [see Figure 8.3]. Look at the field on that card. It's a small scrolling field on a big, mostly blank card. I think that card either needs a picture or to make the field larger so that it takes up more of the card space, or both. It probably wouldn't even have

FIGURE 8.3   Andy's card showing a small field that needlessly scrolls on a mostly blank card.

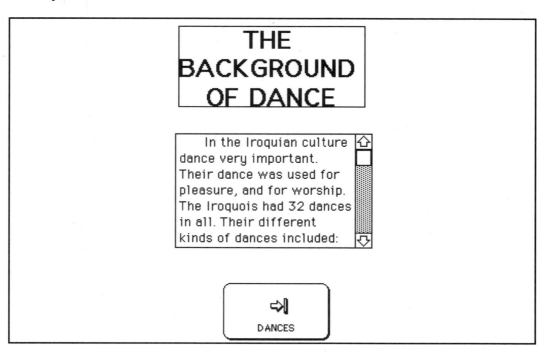

to scroll then. So looking at the scoring guide. I would have to give the stack a score of 8 for card space use. There was more than one card with a space problem in the stack so it can't be Distinguished and there were less than four cards with a space problem so that makes it Competent."

I turned back to Andy. "What do you think about that Andy?" I asked him.

"I see what she means. I made that field scroll just because I think that scrolling a field is fun. But that card and others do seem empty. I really didn't realize that until now," he said.

I complimented Andy on his openness to criticism. "Good, Andy, good. You're once again seeing the benefits that you can gain from an honest, thorough, and fair critique. Remember, you will hurt your friends more if you tell them they have a perfect stack when they don't. Their grade will suffer in the end, and as a result so may your friendship. Remember that our job here as classmates, as it will be in the workplace, is to help everyone produce the best possible product."

Our students seemed to accept this logic. We proceeded through the rest of Andy's stack, evaluating his cards against each separate criterion, and coming to consensus about the level of proficiency for each criterion. We started looking at individual cards, since that was something students had been doing, but quickly shifted gears to how cards worked together and complemented each other, how the cards were linked, and other more holistic and structural concerns. I had the students write suggestions for improvement of the stack on the scoring guide form. We expected that they would do this when they critiqued each other's stacks, so I liked to have them practice as much as possible.

The next day I took my classes to the computer lab to continue to have students practice critiquing. I used the server to put a new stack to critique on each computer so that each student could view and critique the same stack. It could be one from the same class, an anonymous stack from a different class or even year, or one that I created specifically for this purpose.

Each student had a blank scoring guide and the critiquing procedure sheet. I asked the students to critique the stack as we did Andy's before, giving them about ten to fifteen minutes to complete their critiques. After the students were done, we again discussed the critiquing procedure. Next, we discussed how they scored the stack and why they scored it that way. I also asked students to share the suggestions that they wrote on the scoring sheet. Again, we tried to reach some consensus on how the stack should be scored.

Once again we proceeded from teacher-provided assistance, to peer assistance, to the development of self-assisted learning. As students cited details and gave explanations, they were making arguments by making *claims* (the proficiency level citing evidence, for example, "There is blank space") and providing *warrants* (explaining how the card space could have been better used). Throughout this process, as throughout the rest of the project, students were encouraged to make their thinking visible—to articulate what they were thinking and why so that we could "see" it and discuss it as a class.

I knew I was never going to reach 100 percent agreement on scoring a stack. It was clear, however, that we were moving closer toward a community of hypermedia designers with a common set of critical standards. We constantly reminded each other how important this was to what we were doing. Through this process, we helped students develop higher expectations and a new definition of quality work for themselves and their peers.

We were devoted to this cause. The time we spent on the critiquing process was extremely important. We also reminded ourselves of all the skills, knowledge, and attitudes our students were acquiring in the process of completing this project.

After this practice run, we agreed that our students were ready to critique the stacks of peers. We required all students to have their stack critiqued by three other students. For convenience, we had students from their same class hour but a different group critique their stack. We told them that the final assessment of their stack, still to come after a final chance at revision, would come from students outside their own class hour. It was better if the stacks remained anonymous for the final assessment.

The lab was a scene of quiet review and writing as students critiqued each other's stacks. I walked around the lab from computer to computer while students critiqued so that I could help with the occasional indecision that occurred as the students went through stacks. As I walked near Jake, he was talking to himself again.

"I can't believe it!" He sat there shaking his head and mumbling to himself. I asked him if I could help.

"It doesn't make sense. When I push this button to go to the card on religious ceremonies, it makes a belching sound."

I laughed and then asked, "It's not a belching ceremony, is it?"

Jake laughed. "No, it's not."

"Well, I see your problem, Jake. The sound doesn't really fit the purpose of the button, does it?"

Jake looked up at me and said, "Of course, it doesn't fit. What I can't believe is that I didn't think it was funny. A few weeks ago, I would have thought that was really funny. Now the first thing I think is that it's not good! Did you brainwash me or something?"

I knew Jake was kidding, but I could appreciate what he was communicating nonetheless. I answered Jake by saying, "No, I didn't brainwash you, Jake. What I did was help you become an expert on good hypermedia. The fact that you're a smart guy makes you now realize when something is good and when it's not. You probably will still think a belch is funny outside a hypermedia document."

Jake smiled and responded, "Good, you had me worried for a second." Jake then wrote the appropriate suggestions to the author of the stack on the scoring guide and continued to critique the stack.

Students critiqued stacks this way throughout the hour. Each time they completed a critique, they gave the completed scoring guide to the stack's author (see Figure 8.4). The students were instructed to keep all the completed critiques of their stack because we designated on the project checksheet that students would be required to show us the completed critiques. I also told students that it would be interesting to see if these critiques helped to improve the final assessments of their stack, or if they had ignored advice that would have been helpful to them. Since the scoring guide included a spot for the critiquer's name, they would have a record of who said what.

When students had their checklists initialed for three critiques, they were cleared to move on to revising their stacks. I explained to the students that they might not agree with everything the critiquers said but that it was important to remember that their peers were trying to be honest and help them earn the best grade possible.

The best advice I could give them was to read all the critiques carefully and weigh the suggestions. If there was some agreement on the critiques as to how to improve their documents, they should probably make the change. Students also had to weigh the time they had left to complete their individual stacks with the type of changes, revisions, or improvements they wanted to make.

We emphasized that as the author, they had the final decision. On some critique sheets, we included a place for the designer to check whether he accepted, would adapt, or rejected each piece of advice. The designer then had to justify that decision.

Our experience has been that after peer critiques, most students make significant revisions to their stacks—usually regarding linking, card space

Figure 8.4

SCORING GUIDE FOR HYPER PROJECT ASSESSMENT

Disk Number 6786   Hour green   Topic Algonquian   Number of Cards 16   TOTAL POINTS 74
Critiqued by #2163   Education

CRITERIA	DISTINGUISHED	COMPETENT	NOT-YET-COMPETENT	COMMENTS
Multimedia Card Space Justification PTS 10	12 OR 10 PTS 1 bad cd per 10 cds 2 max. Card space has been thoughtfully used and use of multimedia sources has been considered throughout the stack. Author can justify space use if asked. Author has included a properly constructed and meaningful MAP. *good map*	8 PTS 2 bad cds per 10 4 max.	4 PTS 3+ bad cds per 10 5+ total	There was no title on the poem card & on Eders it went off the screen 1 2 3 4 5 6 7 8 9 10
Stack Organization and function PTS 12	12 OR 10 PTS 17+ cds 12-16 cds 11 or less 2 probs. 1 prob. 0 problems Stack organization follows an easy to use Main Menu or Table of Contents card. Organization allows the audience to go through the stack in a way that is informative and makes sense.	8 PTS 17+ cds 12-16 11 or less 3 probs. 2 probs. 1 problem	4 PTS 17+ cds 12-16 cds 11 or less 4+ probs. 3+ probs. 2+ probs.	Every link worked great. The evil spirit thingie was confusing I thought it was a button. 1 2 3 4 5 6 7 8 9 10
Information Quality PTS 10	12 11 10 9 Text is interesting to read and written in the author's own words throughout the stack. There are no gaps in the coverage of the topic or C.F.	8 7 6 5 Most of stack is interesting to read and written in author's own words. Coverage of the topic and C.F. is adequate but could be better.	4 PTS Most of stack is not interesting to read. Much of the text seems to be copied. Topic/C.F. is not covered.	The text was very interesting & caught my intrest.
Spelling and Grammar Quality PTS 10	12 11 10 9 0 1-2 3-4 5 Total errors not more than 1 per cd or maximum of ..... total in stack.	8 7 6 6 7 8 Total errors not more than 2 per cd or a maximum of ... total in stack	4 PTS 9+ ERRORS More than 9 errors.	(Spelling, Capitalization, Punctuation) Run on sentence - mothers / art there. advice - teachers 1 2 3 4 5 6 7 8 9 10
Research Quality PTS 10	12 10 11+ 9-10 Stack contains a bibliography card with different types of sources written in the required format. Points assigned according to Total sources as shown above.	8 5-8	4 PTS < 5	(Books, Encyclopedia, Magazines, Internet, Pamphlet, Interview, CD-ROM, Video) Total Sources = 1 2 3 4 5 6 7 8 9 10
Button Quality PTS 12	12 OR 10 1 PROBLEM PER 5 CDS Reasons for all links and button names are clear and warranted. Author has used icons and effects that help the audience understand stack organization and content.	8 1 PROBLEM PER 3 CDS	4 PTS 2+ PROBS PER 3 CDS	Every button worked 1 2 3 4 5 6 7 8 9 10
Audience Consideration PTS 12	12 10 5+ attempts 4 attempts A variety of attempts have been made throughout the stack to involve the audience in an interesting and engaging way. The stack feels like interactive software.	8 3 attempts to involve audience	4 PTS < 3 attempts	(Pictures 3=1, Animation, Format, Graphic, Quiz, Use Questions, Authentic Sound, Game, Video, Scripted Effects) there were 1 or 2 effects. Really cute pictures & icons

FIGURE 8.4   Student example of scoring guide completed as a critique.

use, and spelling and grammar corrections. Figure 8.5 shows one of the revisions that Andy made to his stack. Clearly, this card is better than its earlier form, shown in Figure 8.3. It is always interesting to see that some of the changes students make to their stacks are not the product of explicit suggestions but of their own observations. They apparently pick up a lot of ideas on how to improve their stack by looking at and critiquing other stacks or by watching others flip through their own stack. This is a bonus of the process.

As students completed the revisions, their individual stack neared completion. Now we asked them to print out their stacks in a reduced size. They cut apart the cards or screens on the printout and pasted them

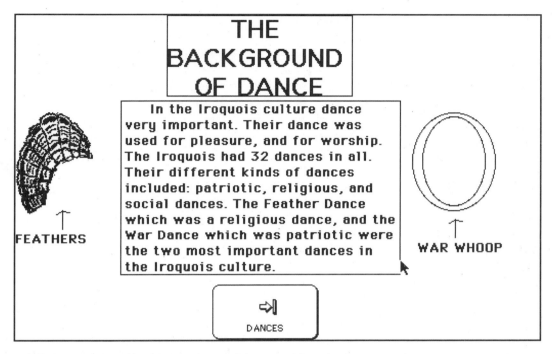

FIGURE 8.5   Andy's card showing revisions and improvements to the card in Figure 8.3.

on construction paper in a way that represented the organization of their stack. Students were required to draw lines between the cards on the paper to show where cards were connected through button links. The result of this activity was a stack printout of a tree or web that would be very similar to the issue trees and webs they had created earlier in the project, when they were organizing and connecting their information. It was always interesting to watch students as they compared these trees or webs and remarked on how their project had taken different twists and turns and finally morphed into its final form.

This activity gives students an opportunity to see a physical representation of what resides as digitized code within their computer. The printouts tend to fall back into the familiar form of the trees or webs students created earlier to represent the organization of their information, but with more associative links within their own stack's structure. Students enjoy comparing their final product to their early plans. As they compare, they are afforded the chance to check whether they have fulfilled their plans. Some students, motivated by their impending presentations at our schoolwide learning fair, would see some final omissions to fill in.

We like to check and discuss these printout trees with students. It's an opportunity to get a quick sense of a student's stack and verify its completeness. We included the printout tree on our checklist to impress on students the importance of completing this step.

Cross-links Between Stacks

Stack printout trees are also useful in the next roundtable discussion. We had students bring their teacher-initialed printout trees to this roundtable activity. Students in each group attached each of their printout trees to a large piece of tagboard. The individually designed hyperstacks were now being combined into one group stack about the culture the group had studied.

We provided each group with colored yarn. The object of the activity was to use the yarn to show the associative connections or cross-links between group members' stacks, with each group member using a different color to show the links she had seen.

This was another activity that was both useful and fun. Students enjoyed putting the yarn on the new giant group tree, and we liked it because students were forced to show the cross-links they had planned in their stacks before they actually made them in the lab. I walked from group to group observing the flurry of activity going on in each one. I stopped at Jenny and Denise's group and looked at the earlier plans the two had made to link their stacks, then interrupted the group with a question. "Did you girls connect your stack as you planned on this earlier stack plan?"

Denise spoke first, "Yes. I have a button on my stack just waiting to be linked to Jenny's card on French history."

Jenny chimed in, "Yeah, and I have a button on my French history card waiting to be connected to Denise's famous portrait card. We have yarn on our group tree that shows these links.

I nodded, "Looking good."

I continued to look at their group tree and noticed several other cross-links established by yarn for other group members. I checked to make sure that they had the buttons on the cards ready to make the proper connection. I looked from face to face around the circle of the group. "Your group has really done a very fine job. But remember that this is a chance to see each member's finished product. Make sure that you take this opportunity to see if there are new cross-links you can make. It's not too late to add more if there is good reason to do so," I told them.

The group nodded in agreement and began to look again at and discuss their stacks. The members took special pride in their individual stacks, but there was also a new attitude clearly visible. The group had taken on a decidedly all-for-one or team flavor. The group cross-linking activity had brought both the individual stacks and the group together and promoted student reflection of the relationships among content.

We shared our stories of the day's group activities. I would love to say that all the groups were as successful as the group with Jenny and Denise in it, but they were not. We always ended up with a few groups in which some members did not meet the due dates or complete their hypermedia document. This was less so than with individual assignments and other projects. It was also the case that students who did not have work done on time were pressured to get it done before the stacks were displayed at our learning fair. Our overall completion rate was as close to perfect as we've ever enjoyed.

Because of the individual-group dynamic, we always weighed each individual's stack more heavily than the group's combined stack, so for some, the group experience was not as pleasant as for others. We considered this a dose of reality. Groups in the workplace are filled with similar problems and dynamics. Students who learned how to work in groups and to weave individual contributions into group projects had learned a valuable life lesson.

The final step that the groups needed to take to complete their project was to link the members' stacks together on the computer. Happily, this step was more inconvenient than hard. I had developed an instruction sheet to lead students through the process of joining their stacks. The process was inconvenient in that each stack had to be loaded onto one computer, so we had to have each stack on a floppy disk and then go through the routine of copying each onto one computer. (This would be much less of a problem in a fully networked lab.)

Once this was accomplished, each group created a stack or card that would function as the title card and central stack menu for the group stack. The group then used the software to link each individual member's stack (main menu card) to a button bearing its name on the central, group stack menu. Each member then made cross-links between stacks as had been planned and discussed. When all of that was accomplished, the group's stack and project was done.

Assessment

We had tried in the past to have teachers evaluate every hypermedia document. Our goal was to have one of us, a resource teacher, or a student teacher (when we had one) sit down with the student author and go through the stack. The teacher evaluators were to discuss the hypermedia document with its author as they used the scoring guide to evaluate it. The biggest advantage to this method was that a teacher was looking at each and every document. The biggest disadvantage was that this took a considerable amount of time. Even using other teachers, it took us many days to go through the 125 or so individual hypermedia documents we had to assess.

We reviewed this method and decided there were other disadvantages. Besides being time-consuming, this method took a lot of energy, and toward the end of the evaluation process, we were not doing as thorough a job. We felt our fatigue caused us to rush through the assessment process as we got to the last students. Another consideration is that we were already familiar with every student's and every group's stack anyway from the constant give and take and daily evaluation throughout the extended project.

In brainstorming to improve this part of the project, we concluded that we needed to get the students as involved in the assessment process as they were in critiquing. We discussed what the downside might be to having students evaluating students and right away identified the privacy issue. There would be many students and parents concerned if the student's grade became public knowledge. We agreed that somehow we needed to hide the identity of the student who made the stack. On the plus side, kids would be continuing to learn from each other.

It turned out that the solution to this challenge was not as difficult as we imagined. Our solution was to assign each student an identification number. Students would use this number to label their disks and their hypermedia documents. If the student kept this number private, there was little chance someone else was going to learn it. So when we began our project that year, we gave each student a number and told them to label their document and disk with it. We also advised them to keep the number a secret.

The system worked well and had a bonus of greatly reducing the acts of vandalism we had experienced in the past. You couldn't see author names on documents or disks, so no person or personality was attached to them. As students moved through the last stages of their project, we were ready to try our peer evaluation process.

Since we had kept the peer critiquing and reviewing process contained in each classroom, we thought it would be better if these same students did not do the evaluating. This did not present a problem because there were plenty of documents to evaluate, and there were plenty of stacks to go around. To help keep the classes' disks separate, I color-coded the disks by hour.

Students would be instructed that they could not evaluate a disk that was the same color as their own hour. Each student would grade five documents using a separate scoring guide for each document. When they had completed the evaluation of a document, they would put their properly filled out scoring guide in a folder bearing the same hour and color as the disk.

Next, the evaluator would check off that he had evaluated that disk on a checksheet (see Figure 8.6) and return the disk to the disk box. The only exception would be if they discovered they were the fifth person to evaluate a disk. That disk would then be given to the teacher, to take it out of circulation. If this process was followed, each student's document would be evaluated five times and no more. Each person would evaluate five stacks, and we would have five scores that we could average to come up with a final score.

We explained the process to each of our classes, and reminded them of the process they had used for critiquing. The evaluation process was essentially the same, but this time the score they aimed at was a bit more permanent. The main thing was to take their time and be fair, honest, and consistent.

As I completed these instructions in Andy's class, his hand shot up. "Yes Andy?"

"What if I don't like the scores that people give me? I worked hard on this, man, and I don't want to get a bad grade just because five idiots grade my stack!" he shot back at me.

I could tell he was truly worried. "I have already considered this," I told him. I directed the rest of my answer to the whole class. "If any of you are unsatisfied with your final average score, you can revise your stack in accordance with the suggestions on your evaluation sheet, and I will regrade it for you."

	A	B	C	D	E	F	G	H
	Disk #	**1st Eval**	**2nd Eval**	**3rd Eval**	**4th Eval**	**5th Eval**	**Average**	
1								
2	1637							
3	971							
4	6347							
5	9386							
6	7347							
7	2255							
8	5502							
9	954							
10	4161							
11	8357							
12	4092							
13	5282							
14	6352							
15	3880							
16	9145							
17	6706							
18	2637							
19	3049							
20	9435							
21	6970							
22	4212							
23	8851							
24	2116							
25	9336							
26								

Table title: Stack Evaluation Check Off Sheet

FIGURE 8.6　**Stack check-off sheet used to keep track of evaluated stacks.**

Andy's hand was up and waving around again. "But, but, but . . ." he stammered.

I cut him off by saying, "If, however, you think that you happened to get five evaluations that were totally unfair, then you can come to one of us and make your case. If we see it your way, we will reevaluate your stack and give you a new grade." (I cannot recall this ever happening—perhaps an indication of how well students have internalized the criteria for the project and how seriously they take their role as evaluators. If you want students to be responsible, give them responsibility. If you want them to be trustworthy, trust them. We were constantly awed at how students often superseded what we thought were already high expectations.)

Andy calmed down and I reemphasized that we wanted them to keep working at their hypermedia documents until they achieved the grade they wanted. Essentially they had until the end of the school year to work on the stacks on their own time if they were really serious about improving their document.

If they did nothing about their grade, then it would stick. The only exception was a failing grade. We did not allow our students to choose to fail. Those students would be required to improve their documents until they were acceptable. I must say how motivation astonishingly improved after only one or two days in our Special Lunch Club. We always told students that it wasn't a punishment, but a way of helping them to be successful in their projects. Our attendees, however, quickly decided they would rather help themselves or be helped during class time and quickly brought their project work up to snuff.

We were pleased with the peer evaluation process. A few stacks were evaluated more than five times, and some students had to evaluate more than five stacks to even things out, but otherwise it went smoothly. It took two days for all the students to complete their five evaluations. As we handed students their average score along with the five peer evaluations, we received very few complaints. We did regrade a number of documents after discussing the evaluations with their authors. We also regraded some documents from students who revised their stacks in an effort to improve their score. The number, however, was a great deal fewer than the 125 or so that we had done in the past.

After debriefing our classes on the process, we decided that there were other advantages to the peer evaluation process. In addition to saving our energy and making students more a part of the process, we saved time.

Probably the biggest additional advantage was the extra learning students did as they evaluated stacks. Time after time, students would excitedly come to us after evaluating a stack and tell us about something interesting that they had just learned. We felt this was the best of both worlds: students were assessing their peers and learning from them at the same time. We had found our evaluation system.

The peer evaluation system worked well, but it is not the only way to evaluate a hypermedia document. Some students chose to monitor for themselves how well their stack taught others by including interactive quizzes in their document that would record audience responses to key questions. Another alternative is to contract with students for their grade.

A simple contract with varying levels of requirements for different grades could be drawn up for students to sign.

The general consensus of our students was that the evaluation process was fair. Students talked about knowing better than us what a typical seventh grader should be able to produce. We didn't argue with them. Students also told us that they felt empowered by the process. The mystery behind grading was gone. Students had developed the standards and applied them to the work of their peers. Students who received low scores still weren't happy, but they had a much harder time finding a peer who was willing to have her shoulder cried upon.

Publication

Andy was literally jumping up and down. "I did it! I did it! We're actually done!" he exclaimed.

I had to laugh at his enthusiastic display. "It's true, Andy, you're done," I confirmed. I told the class that all that was left was to publish their work.

Andy broke in, "How can we publish them? We can't put them in the newspaper or a book."

"You're right, Andy. Those media won't really work for us. But there are ways to publish our projects," I responded.

I went on to remind the class of the many ways Jeff and I had planned for them to share and publish their work. I told them that once the stack evaluations were complete, we would invite the fifth-grade students from the nearby elementary school to sit down and take a look at our work. The neat part was that they would get to act as teachers to these fifth graders. The class broke into a murmur of excitement. I went on to explain that the designers of the stacks would sit behind the fifth graders and answer their questions. This mini–road trip had become something of a tradition in our school district.

The fifth graders were eager for the chance to be in the middle school and talk to future eighth graders. We liked the activity because it helped with fifth-grade transition to sixth grade by creating familiarity and friendships between future sixth- and eighth-grade students. Something like that might even improve the climate of the school—well, a little at least. (We can dream, can't we?)

Another way we would publish the hypermedia documents was to attach them to our school's web page using QuickCard. I told students that on the World Wide Web, there was the potential for a huge audience for their work. We also exchanged the stacks on disks with a partner middle school in another district. We made most of our partnerships through contacts we made at conferences we attended. It was always fun to see what other middle school students were doing and get their feedback on what we had produced.

Other methods of publishing the projects in the past included putting them in the public library, holding a parents' night, sharing them in a learning fair, and submitting them to the state media contest. When we put them in the public library, we would ask the local paper and radio station to make announcements to the public that the student work was there.

The parents' nights had worked quite well the years that we put them together. Students especially enjoyed these nights. Students liked the role reversal, where they were the ones with the knowledge and answers for a change. Parents were always amazed by what their children had produced. The fact that many parents made their feelings of amazement and wonder known to administrators and school board members didn't hurt either. It was a lot easier for our team of teachers to ask for more equipment and computer lab time when parents had already made this case for us.

The learning fair was an evening where the public was invited into our school to see students in the process of learning. One of our best memories is of a senior citizen sitting next to one of our seventh graders and learning HyperCard. By the time they were done, the gentleman had constructed a small stack of his own.

Each time a new audience viewed a stack, students expressed both pride and the desire to do more revisions. When Aaron's mother was flipping through his stack on Rwanda, she noted some spelling errors and also pointed out that events over the past week required that his stack be updated. Aaron quickly unlocked his stack and made the necessary corrections. With hypermedia, revisions are easy, and it made the point to the students that work could always be improved.

The state media contest was another carrot we dangled in front of students to encourage excellence and pride in their work. Our state holds an annual state media fair, with computer-generated media as one of the categories. We tell students that we will submit only the finest hypermedia documents. Many students set their sights on this honor, and it drives them to do their best work. In the absence of a state-level contest, you could create your own contest in your school. The winners' documents could be made the toast of the school.

We put many of the finished products in the library so that they could be used as references. It's also possible to post HyperCard stacks on your web site using programs such as QuickCard and LiveCard.

You may find other new and more innovative ways to publish your students' work. We consider it to be an important part of our project. If we are going to ask students to work hard and do high-quality work, then we should make sure that others see it. When you spend anywhere from eight to twelve weeks on such a project, as we do, the resulting work should be displayed and used. This also reminds student that we learn for real purposes, compose and make things for real audiences, and that knowledge should be made public so that it can be used and extended.

Publishing our students' work makes it more authentic for the students throughout the process. Authentic and public work is work your students too will find worth doing.

Chapter 9

Into the Future

Important Points

This chapter concludes by arguing that this book is not just about technology, as important as learning how to teach with and about technology is coming to be, but even more about powerful teaching and creating powerful learning environments. The projects described in this book, and other projects that would use some of the same processes, are not as complicated or difficult to achieve as one might think. Mostly, it requires a willingness to try.

➡ Students can come to internalize complex repertoires of learning strategies and cognitive skills through long-term projects. They can reach the point where they can do highly sophisticated work autonomously.

➡ You don't need to know much about technology to teach with it. What is much more important and challenging is the need to know kids—how they think and learn—and how to teach them to do and be more than they already are.

➡ You can learn what you need to know about technology from your peers and students, in the context of the projects you pursue together.

➡ Technology can serve as a catalyst to educational change. The rewards of this change are *not* in the technology, but in the possibilities created by teaching well with technology.

➡ Changing schools through project-oriented learning with technology does not require a massive overhaul of curricula, but a rethinking of what is defined as teaching in learning.

➡ Hypertext and electronic technologies are changing the face of literacy. Literacy now must include notions of information access, navigation, selectivity, judgment of reliability, and facility with multiple modes of communication.

➡ Our goal for students should be the achievement of a "literacy of thoughtfulness"—the ability to use various sign systems to serve a variety of human purposes.

➡ Every educational experiment is doomed to succeed! Ask a lot of yourself and your students, and amazing things will happen (and not always exactly the kinds of things you would expect!).

It seems clear to me that children believe in school less and less. This is why disciplinary problems are increasing. School is becoming delegitimized in the eyes of children as they come to see how far it lags behind the society it is supposed to serve, and as they come to understand how backward the ways of learning are that it continues to espouse. *Do we really expect children to sit still for the predigested curriculum of the school when they have known the freedom to explore knowledge on the information highways of the world, and when they have been used to planning complex projects and finding for themselves the knowledge and advice they need to conduct them?*

Seymour Papert (1996, pp. 169–170)

To make a difference, you have to be a doer!

Craig Martin, our eighth-grade teaching colleague

By the fourth quarter of the school year, we had plenty of evidence that our students had internalized the model of student design and could independently use the cognitive skills for research, design, and communication that they had developed during earlier project work.

Our final integrated unit of study during the fourth quarter centered around civil rights and social justice. The student inquiry project for this unit resulted in the creation of a video documentary or a similarly challenging project. We again did some common readings and activities and attempted to arrive at some tentative understandings about our topic. (For an extended discussion of the Space Trader process drama and other activities and readings used to introduce this unit, see Wilhelm and Edmiston 1998.)

As a class, we read Mildred Taylor's (1978) *Roll of Thunder, Hear My Cry,* about a family of color in the Depression-era South, and several other pieces of nonfiction and primary source materials about civil rights issues in America, Asia, and South Africa.

After about three weeks of such study, students began to choose research questions about civil rights or issues of social justice. They pursued their projects during the remainder of the school year, despite the fact that limited class time and very little teacher assistance were provided for this final project. Far from being burned out on design projects, most students seemed more willing and eager to begin a new one than they ever had been before.

At the beginning of the project, questions were critiqued. During the unit, there were occasional group conferences and check-ups. And at the end of the unit, all completed videos were viewed by the class and invited guests. Everything else the groups completed on their own. Although most groups completed a video documentary, some chose to create sophisticated videotaped news magazines, video games, computer games, or dramatic performances to explore their research question on civil rights. Each product represented its newfound understandings to others.

It's important to note that design projects can be created without technology. In fact, many of the drama or museum exhibit projects were fine and showed a sophisticated understanding of research and design skills, as well as conceptual understandings of the explored topic. Still, we would continue to argue that technology provides many features that are naturally motivating and allow students to extend their thinking and knowledge representations.

Teachers and Technology

We really think that teachers don't need to know much about technology. What teachers *do* need to know about is kids—how they learn and think—and how to teach them. As far as technology goes, you need to have a willingness to learn, and to learn particularly willingly from the students. You need to have an inquiring mind, which is exactly what this whole book has argued we must develop in our students. We can hardly develop it if we do not possess and model this capacity ourselves.

Learning technology from the kids (for they will quickly outstrip you, if they have not already) decenters the teacher as a knowledge authority, but it hardly lessens the need students will have of you as a teacher who helps them learn how to learn. This situation places value on students prior and developing knowledge. It privileges them as agents who know and make and learn things. It makes students into teachers. In fact, all of these factors will increase students' need for you, but in a new and nontraditional way of facilitating and assisting their actual learning processes. This is a much more professional and sophisticated pursuit for teachers than delivering information.

In the technological world, good teachers are at a premium, and they are rising like cream to the top of the profession. What these teachers need to know is not a profound understanding of how technology works but about how to teach with it.

It continues to be interesting to us how many students who move on to the eighth grade formally volunteer to help with the next year's seventh-grade projects. And still other former students silently wander into the labs to check things out and find themselves reviewing stacks and providing tutoring for our current students. These scenes always warm our hearts. Our students have become teachers. They learn from each other. And the projects we have pursued together are gripping enough that they continue to work on them or to help others with them long after it is required. This means that the projects are naturally engaging. Although not every student becomes a future peer teacher, all have been pushed to learn and work and communicate to others.

Teaching, assisting others' performances, and giving advice involve as much learning as receiving that assistance. This kind of expert tutoring, process modeling, and the use of last year's documents as models have had interesting and clear effects. Each year's projects get better, in both substance and design. Students see last year's work and create higher critical standards, as witnessed by each year's assessment rubrics. Last year's exception becomes the norm that many students strive to meet and move beyond. (Of course, maybe the improvement is also due to our ever-improving teaching. We can always hope so.)

What we really teach, or need to teach, is how to learn. This includes how to recognize and pose problems, ask questions, find and judge information, and all of the features of student design (see Carver et al. 1992; Erickson 1997; Lehrer 1993; Lehrer et al. 1994). Teaching students how to do these things requires thoughtful pedagogy, task-specific knowledge, and a connected, understanding teacher.

In the past, information could be considered the basis of the curriculum, but that time has passed. Information is not power in the digital age. More information than could possibly be useful in a hundred lifetimes is already immediately available to us. Power is what can be done *with* information: making arguments, connecting different data, perceiving themes, reaching new understandings, providing services that are useful in the real world. Learning to see possibilities and do things with information requires sensitive teaching.

The Urgent Need to Change Schools

More than ever before, we have an open world of opportunity and discovery that will continue to change our world. What will schools do with the technology that is the catalyst of this change? How will schools change to respond to the needs of a changing society?

Many commentators (Lounsbury 1996; Postman 1995; Papert 1996) have argued that schools are by far the most conservative institution in modern society and that they are conserving themselves right out of their usefulness. New demands are being placed on people by their work environment and by the world at large. The faces and demands of literacy have radically multiplied and changed. Schools must respond.

In this regard, we particularly like Seymour Papert's view of microchange and megachange. He defines *microchange* as the low end of the scale, where he places "such 'reforms' as using a word processor for writing assignments and on-line searches for research assignments. These are so minimal that anything short of universal implementation in a country as rich as the U.S. is a national scandal" (1996, p. 156). Although Papert says he does not know what megachange will look like, he does say that "real megachange will come only when most learning is taking place in the course of carrying out challenging projects lasting weeks, months or years" (p. 160). In the context of such projects, technology provides the media and materials for creating learning artifacts and performances, and access to the information students need, when they need it—not when the curriculum says they should need it.

At the heart of such innovative curricula must lie a problem orientation, authentic questions, and the ability to construct knowledge with real people with whom we work and those with whom we work electronically in distant cohorts of learners. As students learn to do these things, they should be given as much responsibility as they can manage to handle, and then provided with scaffolding and other kinds of instruction to help them handle still more. Students learn what we think is important by what we allow them to do. Students learn what they have the opportunity to learn.

A New View of Literacy

In our new technology-rich environment, literacy must be reconceived and its definition broadened. Literacy must now include knowledge of how to access information, navigate hypertexts as readers and as writers, exercise selectivity, and evaluate the reliability of information. This creation and application of critical standards, in one's own work and that of others, must lie at the heart of literacy. Students must learn how to ask: How do I know what I know? How do I know what I know is true and useful?

Literacy, in short, must involve *learning how to learn,* particularly with others. As Papert succinctly puts it: "The only competitive skill in the long run is skill at learning" (1996, p. 166).

Listening, speaking, reading, and writing, as aspects of oral and textual culture, have been shown to develop interdependently, interrelatedly, and concurrently rather than sequentially (Teale and Sulzby 1987). We are sure that this will be found to be true of reading and composing with multimedia as well. Literacy will include reading, learning, and creating meanings with all of the sign systems (icons, video, graphics, drama, animation) that the world affords, and in all combinations.

The ability to use these sign systems, we predict, will be found to develop interrelatedly and concurrently with more traditional literacy skills, such as writing and reading narrative. The field of multimedia composing and reading and how they relate to traditional reading and writing is rich for further research. Our own teacher research, for instance, indicates that multimedia support skill growth and motivation with reluctant readers and reluctant writers.

Literacy events are generally experienced and learned as collaborative, social events. Technology will emphasize the necessity of the social context of literacy. In our own classrooms, projects have promoted a democratic and collaborative culture. Peers assist each other, and all have something to contribute.

Technology will be a force for change in these directions, but there are problems to overcome. Schools must reconceive time and provide longer periods of sustained time for learning. Teachers must rethink teaching. As Tharp and Gallimore argue, a new kind of learning environment "does not require a massive overhaul in curricula. It does, however, require a massive change in what is defined in American schools as teaching" (1990, p. 99).

A Literacy of Thoughtfulness

On the personal bulletin board behind my desk, I (Jeff) have an assortment of messages, Post-it notes, cartoons, and memorabilia. Among them is a yellowed cartoon that shows two kids descending the front steps of a school building. They have dejected faces and heavy book bags. One kid, waving a hand through his hair, says: "I don't get it. They give us worksheets in Reading, English, Math and Social Studies to prepare us for a world of computers, calculators and video."

Next to this cartoon is a quote from Grant Wiggins (1989): "What are the actual performances that we want students to be good at . . . Do we judge our students to be deficient in writing, speaking, listening, artistic creation, research, thoughtful analysis, problem-posing, and problem-solving? [Then] let the tests ask them to write, speak, listen, create, do original research, analyze, pose and solve problems."

Both messages raise several questions about how well we are using school to connect to kids' real concerns and needs and to larger social and cultural purposes that intersect with those needs. How are we working to develop students' meaningful abilities of thought and reflection? How are they working together to do something of significance? What is it, anyway, that these students, future citizens of the twenty-first century, really need to know; what do they really need to be able to do—and why? And how can we best develop these abilities? How can the tasks we do in school be made more authentic and applicable to our students' current concerns and their life outside school?

As teammates teaching seventh grade together, we have described how we considered these questions and how to address them in purposeful, integrated learning situations.

In their National Assessment of Educational Progress report, Kirsch and Jungeblut (1986) relate that although the vast majority of young adults now surpass the literacy standards set three decades ago, at least half of today's students are "midlevel" literates who cannot find information, add to it, connect it to what they already know, transform it, or communicate it to others. In other words, students are not good at finding, connecting, or using information. And if they are given information, they can't *do* anything with it. The information superhighway, with all of its attendant electronic media, can enrich and extend our human abilities to find, link, and use information—but only if we have human purposes for the information and if we know how to perform these complex mental operations in the first place.

To become literate and independent learners, students need to be involved in engaging experiences that will inspire, guide, and scaffold their efforts to learn. The themes of this learning need to include and address the culture of young people and focus on problems and issues situated where young people's personal concerns and larger social concerns intersect (Beane 1990). We believe that learning should be integrated around a problem-centered core that speaks to the lives lived by students, not organized by arbitrary subject divisions, which is the case in nearly all schools.

Literacy was once considered the ability to read and write at a functional level. With the demands of our modern technological world, this definition of literacy is insufficient. We need a new definition of literacy that Brown (1992) calls a "literacy of thoughtfulness." This new definition "expands the traditional concept of literacy, as a simple decoding process, by making it inseparable from a number of complicated thinking activities which take place in contexts of personal and social purpose" (p. 32). When Brown interviewed experts on literacy, they told him that literacy now means the ability to think, to think about thinking, to dialogue with the past and with others, to find and solve problems, and to use technology to extend our abilities to do all of these things.

It has become clear to us that the technology of hypermedia can provide a format for encouraging students to develop a literacy of thoughtfulness and providing media in which to be actively engaged with information, for creating and linking information and—perhaps most important—for providing a guide and support as students pursue a variety of thinking processes.

Papert tells us that schools are conservative organisms that protect themselves from change, and that "education bureaucrats are specialists in conservatism and inaction" (1996, p. 164). Still, he believes that with the new wave of Internet access, perhaps innovation can go over the hump and resist the backsliding toward more traditional curricula that has been inevitable in the past. We hope that projects such as our own will help to be part of this movement of change.

Something Ventured, Something Learned

What Did the Students Learn?

All of our students learned how to use, read, and design hypermedia documents. This in itself may be a worthy achievement. Bolter (1991) argues that hypertext is superseding the book as our primary text. As a major communication tool of the future, hypertext will have far-reaching consequences for how we organize information, read, write, and think of literacy.

At the end of each year, our students were able to use hypermedia to find information electronically and to organize and link information, literacy skills that are already of daily importance to them. They also began to develop critical standards for the relevance, appropriateness, and organization of text and began to construct much more active and participatory roles for themselves as authors and readers.

We believe, and have begun to establish more formally, that the hypermedia projects helped them to explore and remember content information about characters, and psychological or cultural topics of their choice.

And the students now knew how to pursue their own learning. As Jordan told us: "I used to think research was something really hard, and I would never want to even get started on it. Now I know I can do it. I know *how* to do it." And so did our other students, as evidenced by their year-ending work.

What Did the Teachers Learn?

We learned that if you have a theory of learning, you need to explore ways of implementing it. Technology can help teachers to do this. Once implementing a new means of supporting student learning, you need to stick with it and let students work with it over and over again. Using technology, like trying anything else new in the classroom, is challenging, but great rewards are possible. And it's important to emphasize that the rewards are not in the technology; the rewards are in the possibilities one can create when using technology to restructure learning.

We asked ourselves: Have we ever had 100 percent enthusiastic participation and completion of final projects before? Never. Have our struggling students, like Jordan, ever been able to choose a topic, find information about it, organize and represent that information to others before, and in such a short time? Never. We've discussed at length how it took Jordan a whole school year of hard work to achieve what he did—something that he recognized himself as being superior work when he told us: "This [final exam] is the best thing I've ever wrote."

Was it easy? Was it a wonder method? No. But the course of true learning never did run smooth. We just thought that hypermedia helped it to run a little more smoothly and a lot further.

We proved to ourselves that if you want students to read, write, and think and be able to use technology, then you aim at their higher-level mental processes as you ask them to do so. When you ask them to "make" things that will be read and used by others, they take the task seriously.

Seymour Papert refers to this kind of learning as "hard fun." We certainly found that the kinds of challenges presented by inquiry and hypermedia design engaged and excited our students.

Were we happy with our units during the first year or even during this latest year? No. We are constantly tinkering and reworking our projects—always anticipating the arrival of the next year's students. And we feel a little bit like Tennyson's Ulysses as we do so: sailing off into the hypertextual future with our students, where great, undreamed-of deeds may yet be done.

Works Cited

Bakhtin, M. 1986. *Speech Genres and Other Late Essays.* Trans. Vern McGee. Austin, TX: University of Texas Press.

Beane, J. 1990. *A Middle School Curriculum: From Rhetoric to Reality.* Columbus, OH: National Middle School Association.

Bloom, B. 1976. *Human Characteristics and School Learning.* New York: McGraw-Hill.

————, ed. 1985. *Developing Talent in Young People.* New York: Ballantine.

Bolter, J. D. 1991. *Writing Space: The Computer, Hypertext, and the History of Writing.* Hillsdale, NJ: Lawrence Erlbaum.

Brazee, E., and J. Capelluti. 1995. *Dissolving Boundaries: Toward an Integrative Curriculum.* Columbus, OH: National Middle School Association.

Brown, A. L. 1997. Transforming Schools into Communities of Thinking and Learning About Serious Matters. *American Psychologist* 52: 399–413.

Brown, A. L., and J. C. Campione. 1994. Guided Discovery in a Community of Learners. In K. McGilly, ed., *Classroom Lessons: Integrating Cognitive Theory and Classroom Practice,* pp. 229–270. Cambridge, MA: MIT Press/Bradford Books.

————. 1996. Psychological Theory and the Design of Innovative Learning Environments: On Procedures, Principles, and Systems. In L. Schauble and R. Glaser, eds., *Innovations in Learning: New Environments for Education,* pp. 289–325. Hillsdale, NJ: Lawrence Erlbaum.

Brown, R. 1992. *Schools of Thought.* San Francisco: Jossey-Bass.

Bruer, J. T. 1993. *Schools for Thought.* Cambridge, MA: MIT Press.

Byrnes, J. P. 1996. *Cognitive Development and Learning in Instructional Contexts.* Boston: Allyn & Bacon.

Carver, S., R. Lehrer, T. Connell, and J. Erickson. 1992. Learning by Hypermedia Design: Issues of Assessment and Implementation. *Educational Psychologist* 27, 3: 385–404.

Clark, E. 1997. *Designing and Implementing an Integrated Curriculum: A Student-Centered Approach.* Brandon, VT: Holistic Education Press.

Cognition and Technology Group at Vanderbilt. 1994. From Visual Word Problems to Learning Communities: Changing Conceptions of Cognitive Research. In K. McGilly, ed., *Classroom Lessons: Integrating Cognitive Theory and Classroom Practice,* pp. 157–200. Cambridge, MA: MIT Press/Bradford Books.

Collins, A., J. S. Brown, and S. E. Newman. 1989. Cognitive Apprenticeship: Teaching the Crafts of Reading, Writing, and Mathematics. In L. B. Resnick, ed., *Knowing, Learning, and Instruction: Essays in Honor of Robert Glaser,* pp. 453–494. Hillsdale, NJ: Lawrence Erlbaum.

Csikszentmihalyi, M. 1990. *Flow: The Psychology of Optimal Experience.* New York: Harper & Row.

Csikszentmihalyi, M., and R. Larson. 1984. *Being Adolescent: Conflict and Growth in the Teenage Years.* New York: Basic Books.

Csikszentmihalyi, M., K. Rathunde, and S. Whalen. 1993. *Talented Teenagers: The Roots of Success and Failure.* Cambridge, UK: Cambridge University Press.

DeBevois, S. 1991. Applications MegaMedia: The Future, Soon. *IBM Multimedia: Supplement to the T.H.E. Journal* (September): 10–11.

Dewey, J. 1910. *How We Think.* Boston: Heath.

diSessa, A. 1992. Images of Learning. In E. DeCorte, M. Linn, H. Mandl, and L. Verschaffel, eds., *Computer-Based Learning Environments and Problem-Solving,* pp. 19–40. NATO Series ASI Series F. New York: Springer-Verlag.

Edmiston, B. 1991. What have you travelled? A teacher researcher study of structuring drama for reflection. Unpublished doctoral dissertation, Ohio State University, Columbus, OH.

Erickson, J. 1997. Building a Community of Designers: Restructuring Learning Through Student Hypermedia Design. *Journal of Research in Rural Education* 13, 1: 5–27.

Erickson, J., and R. Lehrer. In press. The Evolution of Critical Standards as Students Design Hypermedia Documents. *Journal of the Learning Sciences* (special issue on learning through problem solving).

Fosnot, C. T. 1996. *Constructivism: Theory, Perspectives, and Practice.* New York: Teachers College Press.

Goodlad, J. 1984. *A Place Called School.* New York: McGraw-Hill.

Gould, J. S. 1996. A Constructivist Perspective on Teaching and Learning in the Language Arts. In C. T. Fosnot, ed., *Constructivism: Theory, Perspectives, and Practice,* pp. 92–102. New York: Teachers College Press.

Greene, M. 1978. *Landscapes of Learning.* New York: Teachers College Press.

Harel, I. 1991. *Children Designers: Interdisciplinary Constructions for Learning and Knowing Mathematics in a Computer-Rich School.* Norwood, NJ: Ablex.

Harel, I., and S. Papert, eds. 1991. *Constructionism.* Norwood, NJ: Ablex.

Hayes, J., and L. Flower. 1980. Identifying the Organization of Writing Processes. In L. Gregg and E. Steinberg, eds., *Cognitive Processes in Writing: An Interdisciplinary Approach,* pp. 3–30. Hillsdale, NJ: Lawrence Erlbaum.

Heath, S., and M. McLaughlin. 1993. *Identity and Inner-City Youth: Beyond Ethnicity and Gender.* New York: Teachers College Press.

Heathcote, D., and G. Bolton. 1995. *Drama and Learning: Dorothy Heathcote's Mantle of the Expert Approach to Education.* Portsmouth, NH: Heinemann.

Hillocks, G., Jr. 1995. *Teaching Writing as Reflective Practice.* New York: Teachers College Press.

Julyan, C., and E. Duckworth. 1996. A Constructivist Perspective on Teaching and Learning Science. In C. T. Fosnot, ed., *Constructivism: Theory, Perspectives, and Practice,* pp. 55–72. New York: Teachers College Press.

Katz, L., and S. Chard. 1989. *Engaging Children's Minds: The Project Approach.* Norwood, NJ: Ablex.

Kirsch, I., and A. Jungeblut. 1986. *Literacy: Profiles of America's Young Adults.* Princeton, NJ: National Assessment of Educational Progress.

Lehrer, R. 1993. Authors of Knowledge: Patterns of Hypermedia Design. In S. Lajoie and S. Derry, eds., *Computers as Cognitive Tools,* pp. 197–227. Hillsdale, NJ: Lawrence Erlbaum.

Lehrer, R., J. Erickson, and T. Connell. 1994. Learning by Designing Hypermedia Documents. In W. M. Reed, J. K. Burton, and M. Liu, eds., *Multimedia and Megachange: New Roles for Educational Computing,* pp. 227–254. New York: Haworth Press.

Lounsbury, J. 1996. We now know the cure. Speech delivered to the Maine Middle Level Institute, Orono, ME, April.

Mercer, N. 1995. *The Guided Construction of Knowledge.* Adelaide, Australia: Multilingual Matters.

National Association of Secondary School Principals. 1996. *Breaking Ranks: Changing an American Institution.* Reston, VA: NASSP.

Negroponte, N. 1995. *Being Digital.* New York: Vintage.

Newkirk, T. 1992. Silences in Our Teaching Stories. In T. Newkirk, ed., *Workshop 4: Teacher Research,* pp. 21–30. Portsmouth, NH: Heinemann.

Ogle, D. 1983. K-W-L Plus: A Strategy for Comprehension and Summarization. *Journal of Reading* 30, 7: 626–631.

Papert, S. 1996. *The Connected Family.* Atlanta, GA: Longstreet Press.

Penner, D., N. Giles, R. Lehrer, and L. Schauble. 1997. Building Functional Models: Designing an Elbow. *Journal of Research in Science Teaching* 34, 2: 125–143.

Perkins, D. N. 1986. *Knowledge as Design.* Hillsdale, NJ: Lawrence Erlbaum.

Postman, N. 1992. *Technopoly: The Surrender of Culture to Technology.* New York: Vintage.

———. 1995. *The End of Education: Redefining the Value of School.* New York: Knopf.

Power, B., J. Wilhelm, and K. Chandler. 1997. *Reading Stephen King: Issues of Censorship, Student Choice, and the Canon.* Urbana, IL: National Council of Teachers of English.

Raphael, T. 1982. Question Answering Strategies for Children. *Reading Teacher* 36, 2: 186–190.

Renzulli, J. 1976. The Enrichment Triad Model: A Guide for Developing Defensible Programs for the Gifted and Talented. *Gifted Child Quarterly* 20, 3: 303–326.

Resnick, M., and S. Ocko. 1990. LEGO/Logo: Learning Through and About Design. In I. Harel, ed., *Constructionist Learning: A 5th Anniversary Collection of Papers,* pp. 121–128. Cambridge, MA: MIT Media Lab.

Rogoff, B. 1990. *Apprenticeship in Thinking.* New York: Oxford University Press.

Scardamalia, M., and C. Bereiter. 1992. Text-Based and Knowledge-Based Questioning by Children. *Cognition and Instruction* 9, 3: 177–199.

Shifter, D. 1996. A Constructivist Perspective on Teaching and Learning Mathematics. In C. T. Fosnot, ed., *Constructivism: Theory, Perspectives, and Practice,* pp. 73–91. New York: Teachers College Press.

Siu-Runyan, Y., and V. Faircloth. 1995. *Beyond Separate Subjects: Integrative Learning at the Middle Level.* Norwood, MA: Christopher-Gordon.

Smagorinsky, P., and J. Coppock. 1994. Cultural Tools and the Classroom Context: An Exploration of an Alternative Response to Literature. *Written Communication* 11, 3: 283–310.

Stiggins, R. 1987. Measuring Thinking Skill Through Classroom Assessment. ERIC Document 290761, November.

Taylor, M. 1978. *Roll of Thunder, Hear My Cry!* New York: Dial.

Teale, W., and E. Sulzby. 1987. Emergent Literacy: Writing and Reading. ERIC Document 280004.

Tharp, R. G., and R. Gallimore. 1990. *Rousing Minds to Life: Teaching, Learning and Schooling in Social Context.* Cambridge, UK: Cambridge University Press.

von Glasersfeld, E. 1996. Aspects of Constructivism. In C. T. Fosnot, ed., *Constructivism: Theory, Perspectives, and Practice,* pp. 3–7. New York: Teachers College Press.

Vogt, L. 1985. Comprehension Teaching Strategies to Bridge Home and School Language. In G. Speidel, ed., *Oral Language in a Successful Reading Program for Hawaiian Children,* pp. 74–94. Honolulu: Kamehameha Schools/Bishop Estate, Center for Development of Early Education.

Vygotsky, L. S. 1978. In M. Cole, V. John-Steiner, S. Scribner, and E. Souberman, eds. and trans., *Mind in Society: The Development of Higher Psychological Processes.* Cambridge, MA: Harvard University Press.

Wiggins, G. 1989. Teaching to the (Authentic) Test. *Educational Leadership* 9: 41–47.

Wigginton, E. 1986. *Sometimes a Shining Moment: The Foxfire Experience.* Garden City: Anchor Books.

Wilhelm, J. 1996. *Standards in Practice: Grades 6–8.* Urbana, IL: National Council of Teachers of English.

———. 1997. *You Gotta BE the Book: Teaching Engaged and Reflective Reading with Adolescents.* New York: Teachers College Press.

Wilhelm, J., and B. Edmiston. 1998. *Imagining to Learn: Inquiry, Ethics, and Integration Through Drama.* Portsmouth, NH: Heinemann.

Williams, S. M., R. Bareiss, and B. J. Reiser. 1996. ASK Jasper: A multimedia publishing and performance support environment for design. Paper presented at the Annual Meeting of the American Educational Research Association, New York, April.

Winn, W. 1989. Toward a Rational and Theoretical Basis for Educational Technology. *Educational Technology Research and Development* 37, 1: 35–46.

Wood, K. 1997. *Interdisciplinary Instruction: A Practical Guide for Elementary and Middle School Teachers.* Columbus, OH: Prentice-Hall.